WETLANDS

WETLANDS

Text and Photography by

David J. Hawke

Stoddart

A BOSTON MILLS PRESS BOOK

Dedication

This book is dedicated to all who have shared their knowledge of wetlands,

in particular to Fran Westman, naturalist and inspiration,

and to the memory of Lloyd Cook, trapper and teacher,

and to my daughters, Erin and Shannon, who are also my teachers and my inspiration.

Canadian Cataloguing in Publication Data
Hawke, David J.
    Wetlands

ISBN 1-55046-046-3

1. Wetlands - Ontario. 2. Wetland flora - Ontario. 3. Wetland fauna - Ontario. 4. Wetlands - Ontario - Pictorial works. 5. Wetland flora - Ontario - Pictorial works. 6. Wetland fauna - Ontario - Pictorial works. I. Title.

QH541.5.M3H38 1993   574.5'26325'09713   C92-093915-5

First published in 1994 by
Stoddart Publishing Co. Limited
34 Lesmill Road
Toronto, Canada
M3B 2T5
(416) 445-2333

A BOSTON MILLS PRESS BOOK
The Boston Mills Press
132 Main Street
Erin, Ontario
N0B 1T0

Design by Mary Firth

The publisher gratefully acknowledges the support of The Canada Council, Ontario Ministry of Culture and Communications, Ontario Arts Council, and Ontario Publishing Centre in the development of writing and publishing in Canada.

PRINTED AND BOUND IN HONG KONG
BY BOOK ART INC., TORONTO

Contents

Perhaps the concept of day care originated with Canada geese, since broods join together as soon as the goslings can swim! Adults take turns herding the youngsters—an arduous task in high grass but an easy one on the quiet open water because goslings follow anything that is tall and black and white.

The deep, quiet ponds behind mills and beaver dams are the preferred habitat of bullfrogs. As mill ponds are drained, and acid precipitation increases the pH of remaining ponds, this amphibian will no longer be the common species it once was. The booming calls of bullfrogs have already ceased in several regions.

Beaver ponds are tranquil wetlands that sustain many types of plants and wildlife. Water-lily leaves cool the shallow waters with their shade and provide a resting spot for innumerable invertebrates, both above and below the water surface.

Preface

As a naturalist, I have had the good fortune of working at the education centres located on two well-known wetland sites in southern Ontario: Wye Marsh and Tiny Marsh. This experience, which has spanned fourteen years, has allowed me to both learn and teach about wetlands on a very intimate level.

Being involved with public education and nature-awareness programs, I find it unsettling that the general public is largely uninformed about the roles that wetlands play in sustaining our lives. It is my hope that this book will help promote a better understanding of the importance of these disappearing marshes, swamps, bogs, and fens, not only to wildlife, but to people, as well.

A drawback to having marshes such as Tiny and Wye presented as "showpieces" is that some people feel these few protected areas are all that is needed to preserve our wetland heritage; visitors come, see wildlife, and return to their homes thinking that all is well in the world of wetlands. However, most of the wetlands surrounding the lower Great Lakes have been destroyed (up to eighty-three percent by some estimates), and the remaining few are still under threat of being drained, filled, or polluted.

In the past, wetlands have been maligned, misunderstood, and mismanaged. Today—at long last—they are being studied, rejuvenated, and intensively managed, for they are now recognized as the most precious habitat to be found in the Great Lakes area.

The images and words in this book are meant to encourage everyone to act now to save and protect our remaining wetlands, to keep them from becoming an endangered habitat.

Raindrops on fallen aspen leaves

FACING PAGE: Tiny Marsh

Yellow lady's-slipper orchids

Acknowledgments

Knowing full well that I will probably overlook someone (and I apologize right now if I do), I would like to make special mention of the people who have had an impact both on this book and its author.

My parents, John and Gwen, who have always encouraged me to do my best, to follow my interests in nature, and who have provided many opportunities for these interests to grow.

My co-workers at the Wye Marsh Wildlife Centre (1979 to 1985) and the Tiny Marsh Provincial Wildlife Area (1985 to 1992); in particular, Bob Whittam, Eva Kaiser, and Andy Fletcher.

Paul McKerroll, Randy Turner, and John Lahay, who have shared many outdoor adventures with me in wetlands of all descriptions.

Kathy MacDonald-Novak, a kindred spirit who knows the joy of slogging through a bog, and Christopher Chenier, amiable wetland adventurer.

My fellow naturalists in the Brereton, Midland, and Orillia naturalists' clubs; in particular, Fran Westman, Luke Irwin, Bill Cattley, Fred Noakes, and Anne Hughes, all wonderful teachers and field companions.

Organizations and agencies such as Ducks Unlimited, The Nature Conservancy of Canada, Federation of Ontario Naturalists, Ontario Federation of Anglers and Hunters, Environment Canada, Wildlife Habitat Canada, Natural Heritage League, and the Ontario Ministry of Natural Resources, whose combined efforts are helping to save wetlands for the future.

John Denison, Noel Hudson, and Gillian Stead of Boston Mills Press, for their enthusiasm for this project and their encouragement, and for their honest opinions, given despite the duress of recession, reorganization, and renovation.

Juliana—wife, artist, homemaker, and friend—for her unwavering support and understanding.

And to those whose names I've missed here, thank you for your friendship and for all you have taught me in regards to understanding wetlands.

Introduction

L et's start with a word-association exercise. What mental image (or emotion) do you experience when you read the word bog? Swamp? Marsh?

For "bog," I envision a riot of colours: pink, blue, green, purple, white. All are colours of the flowers, trees, bark, lichens, and mosses of a bog.

For "swamp," I picture a world of green: green leaves, green moss, green canopy, green algae, green duckweed; and trees, living and dead, with birds searching out hidden insects.

For "marsh," I see towering cattails, open patches of water, ducks in flight, and hear a symphony of noises coming from behind the close green walls of vegetation.

Unfortunately, for wetlands, not everyone shares my point of view. Bogs are often thought of as mysterious, cold, wet places which envelope any man or beast foolish enough to come near them. Swamps are where strange creatures live amongst hordes of disease-ridden insects and heavy, foul air. Marshes are usually seen as places where tractors get stuck in the mud.

Wetlands definitely have an image problem. And that's a shame, as they are areas of great importance both to wildlife and people.

Since explorers and settlers first came to Canada, wetlands have been looked upon as places to avoid or conquer. Unless the swamps and marshes could be drained or filled they were considered worthless areas, a blight upon what might have otherwise been good farmland.

The attitude that "wetlands are wastelands" has been ingrained in generations of people. Even today, in the "environmentally aware" era of the '90s, many people still have no idea of the role and value of wetlands.

I believe that, to make something happen, the three A's must be followed: Awareness, Appreciation, and Action. It is my hope that this book will make you more aware of the importance of wetlands, that you will come to appreciate them, and that you will be inspired to take action to help protect and save the few wetlands that remain.

Most of our wetlands in southern Ontario have already been destroyed (estimates usually range

Just as cattails are the best-known wetland plants, red-winged blackbirds are the most renowned bird species. Males are noisy and brightly coloured to defend territorial boundaries and to attract females; the females are mainly quiet and dull brown, too busy raising their young to argue over who owns which cattail.

FACING PAGE: *Marshes are the most easily recognized wetland in the lower Great Lakes region. These open patches of shallow water surrounded by dense stands of cattails are home to hundreds of species of wildlife.*

Often feared because movies have portrayed them as such eerie places, swamps are actually fascinating areas to explore. The dominant vegetation is trees, both living and dead, which provide shade, food, and shelter to wood ducks, woodpeckers, raccoons, bats, tree swallows, and chickadees.

The thick, lush growth found in a wetland creates and stores energy from sunlight more efficiently than any other habitat. As wetland plants are eaten, this stored energy is transferred to animals, which in turn may be eaten by other animals. However, the invasion of purple loosestrife is upsetting this diverse and delicate system.

from seventy-five to eighty-three percent). In the past this was done out of ignorance. Today we are *still* destroying our precious wetlands, but now it is done for short-sighted greed, by those who have bought cheaply priced land and hope to fill it in and make it "valuable" land.

However, as wetlands are converted into sites for parking lots, video rental stores, and fast food outlets, the public must pay real dollars for water quality improvement, erosion control, flood control, groundwater recharge, sedimentation control, and fish and wildlife habitat improvement—all of which normally are provided by wetlands.

Chief Dan George is credited for the following quote, one which I feel captures the attitude of why our wetlands are still being destroyed:

> "When you talk with the animals, they will talk with you and you will understand each other.
> If you do not talk with the animals, you will not understand them.
> What Man does not understand, he fears.
> What Man fears, he destroys."

Wetlands protection must be given priority in all development plans, at all levels of government. We must learn how to live with nature, even if only for our own benefit. Wise and informed choices must be made to regulate our use of the remaining wetlands, because they are irreplaceable. Wetlands are one of our most needed and least understood natural resources.

Wetlands often are called "Nature's nursery" because many species of wildlife begin their lives within the wet confines of a marsh or swamp. Some creatures will spend their entire lives here; others leave as they mature.

Existing wetlands can be enhanced but attempts to create wetlands have failed. And the world's water supply is finite. Water can change states, from liquid to gas to solid, but remains essentially the same water. Whatever was here in the beginning is still with us today. The water that recently fell as rain, or is held in a wetland, or comes from your faucet is the same water that dinosaurs wallowed in and the Vikings sailed upon.

While we can't create or destroy water, we can certainly alter its flow, location, and purity. And herein lies the problem

16

facing us at present: as wetland habitat is lost, the new patterns of water flow do not allow the remaining wetlands to function as they should.

There are many people who love wetlands. To them the calls of red-winged blackbirds and spring peepers are as soothing as fine music; the soaring, swooping flocks of foraging shorebirds are a graceful ballet; and cattail leaves swaying in a warm summer's breeze create a sensation of wellness and peace. The soft embrace of the wetlands' lush vegetation welcomes them into the well-ordered world of nature.

Marsh marigold buds are edible when the plant first emerges in the spring. As the plant matures and blossoms, toxins within make it unfit to eat. Honey bees, however, delight in visiting the showy blooms.

DEFINITIONS

WETLAND: an area which is wet all or part of the year and which supports the type of vegetation and aquatic life that requires wet or seasonally wet conditions for growth and reproduction.

HABITAT: a place which offers living things a combination of food, water, shelter, and space in the amounts needed to survive.

TYPES OF WETLANDS

There are many types of wetlands in the Great Lakes region, the five most common types being:

MARSHES: water flows through a vegetation community consisting mainly of cattails

SWAMPS: water flows through a vegetation community dominated by trees, both living and dead

BOGS: water is stagnant, or nearly so, usually with an acidic pH, and has a specialized plant community

FENS: water seeps slowly through a dense layer of poorly decayed vegetation, usually found on a base of limestone or clay

SHORELINE: thick stands of bulrushes, reeds, or cattails break wave action and protect fragile shorelines of lakes and rivers

VALUE OF WETLANDS

1. Food webs and food chains. Any food web or food chain will contain species that depend upon wetlands for a portion or all of their lives. More than twice as many threatened or endangered species are associated with wetlands than with any other habitat.

2. Waterfowl. Of all the ducks and geese which are hatched in North America, seventy percent start in a wetland in Canada.

*A least bittern peers out from behind a
clump of cattails and bulrushes.
Difficult to see even at the best of times
because it is shy and well-camouflaged,
this bird is one of several rare species
that call a wetland "home."*

3. Fish. Many species of fish must reach flooded wetlands to spawn. The young fish will stay in the protected shallows until they are ready to move into the larger lakes.

4. Furbearers. Most of the more valuable furs are from mammals which live in the wetlands: beaver, mink, otter, and muskrat.

5. Flood control. Wetlands retain water from snowmelt and heavy rainfall. This water is released into the watershed, but on a gradual basis.

6. Erosion control. As flowing water enters a wetland, it spreads out and slows down, thereby reducing the friction on streambanks and roadside ditches.

7. Filtration. Sediment is removed from the water when the water velocity drops in a wetland. Plants physically screen some of the larger pieces from the water; nutrients and even heavy metals are absorbed by the plants.

The acidic water found in bogs limits the variety of plants that can survive there. Tamarack trees, which blaze golden in the autumn as they lose their needles, are one species that prefers bog or bog-like soil conditions.

8. Cooling system. Water which seeps underground through a swamp or marsh is cooled before returning to the main flow.

9. Groundwater supply. Underground water tables are maintained with the water which is held and slowly released from within wetlands.

10. Productivity. Wetlands rival the yield of modern agricultural fields, which require intensive cultivation and fertilization each year. Wetlands are quite similar to rain forests in their ability to turn solar energy into biomass.

11. Resource use. Wetlands attract users of many types: canoeists, photographers, hunters, trappers, anglers, naturalists, researchers, and educators. In Ontario, over $800 million are spent each year by people pursuing a wetland activity. In Michigan, each wetland acre has a potential income of $500 per acre for the state.

12. Aesthetic value. Wetlands are pleasing to look at and enhance our quality of life.

Heralds of Spring

Winter is a time of unmatched beauty, yet the short days, long, cold nights, and limited variety of observable wildlife wear on even the hardiest naturalist. Throughout the dreary month of March, however, there are unmistakable signs of seasonal change that lift even the lowest spirits.

Just yesterday dead cattails stretched from the shoreline, silent and stark against the dirty snow and greying ice. But today, despite stinging snowflakes blown by a biting wind, a red-winged blackbird sits singing on top of a weathered cattail stalk, his proud, raspy song marking the borders of his summer territory. Soon there will be so many others that his presence will hardly be noteworthy. But for now, his is the only voice heard in the frozen marshland. Today he is the first, the harbinger of good news— spring is coming!

There may be a few more snowfalls, but they will be the last of the long winter assault. That grating *o-ka-ree* announces that the seasons are changing. Soon the warmer weather will be upon us, proclaims the blackbird.

Tomorrow two or three more of these songsters, all male, will be scattered among the beaten cattails, jousting like black knights, with their boastful calls and their flashy red emblems.

The brown-and-white striped females won't arrive until April. By then the males will have their territories defined, the ice will have melted, and food will be more plentiful. Depending on the size of a male's territory and his aggressiveness, he may entice three or more females to live with him. Every so often a neighbouring male will slip across the boundary and mate with one of the females next door, before quietly returning to his own harem.

But today the females are still hundreds of kilometres to the south and a lone male sings in the biting snow.

FACING PAGE: Spring run-off creates floods along many rivers, especially those that no longer have wetlands to absorb the overflow. Common mergansers, usually found on open water, will visit flooded areas in search of fish and frogs to eat.

The cold, often wet weather of March does not deter the male red-winged blackbird from returning to his favourite marsh. The older birds arrive first and claim the choicest areas ahead of the younger, inexperienced males. Females appear when the ice breaks up in early April.

With the ducks comes the duck hawk, better known as the peregrine falcon. Waterfowl are a favourite menu item of these falcons, but with harmful consequences. Chemicals flushed into the wetlands are ingested by invertebrates; ducks eat these small animals and store the chemicals in their fat; falcons eat the ducks, and the accumulated chemicals cause the falcons to produce eggs with thin or non-existent shells that fail to hatch. As a result the falcon population has plummeted dangerously low and the peregrine falcon is now an endangered species.

He is probably an older male who has nested here before, and he knows that food and shelter are good in this marsh. By arriving ahead of the others, he ensures that what was his last year remains his this year, too.

The swirling late-winter snowfall is heavier now, but filtering through the thick veil of snow, echoing off the dead ash trees, comes a sound other than the red-winged blackbird's song. A moment of silence, then I hear it again. Drifting down through the cloud bank, trumpeting their own arrival, comes a pair of Canada geese. They drop low and fly past the thick brush on the shore, circling the still-frozen marsh, then, with great fanfare, settle on the ice to reacquaint themselves with their summer home. They bob their heads and shake their necks excitedly, but their furtive glances toward the brushy shoreline betray their concern that no open water is available.

Eventually they lift off to visit other places and deliver the message that spring is on its way. But they'll be back, when the sun shines brighter and the winds blow warmer, when the eons-old instinct to begin nesting takes hold of them in a way they cannot ignore.

As I stand beside the marsh, the snowflakes stinging my face and the wind finding its way around my collar, I am happy. Spring is coming, just as it has to this marsh for the past ten thousand years. And this year I was here on the day the heralds of spring appeared.

One of the last wetland inhabitants to return in the spring is the blue-winged teal, a small duck that winters on the Caribbean islands of Jamaica, Cuba, Trinidad, and Haiti. The males have a distinctive white slash on their faces. Both sexes have powder-blue wing patches.

Sunrise Canoeing

The summer marsh waits calm and quiet in the pre-dawn light, its surface like molten silver. It mirrors perfectly the soft pink tinge of the scattered clouds that hang overhead.

I walk the short trail from my car to the shoreline, and carefully set my knapsack in the waiting canoe, impatient to get under way.

I step gingerly into the canoe, trying to keep noise to a minimum, and bump the paddle against the thwarts only twice. The resounding *clunks* sound like rolls of thunder in the stillness, but none of the marsh inhabitants protest.

A hearty push against the grassy bank and a swoosh of the ash paddle through the floating water lily leaves, and I am off. This gentle paddle-about will add another day to the long association between canoes and marshes. The canoe was originally created as a means of transportation through these inter-connecting shallow lakes. Today it is used mainly for recreational pursuits—a medium for enchanted exploration.

An occasional muted splash from within the thick stands of translucent green cattails stirs my curiosity and spurs my sense of discovery. Time and social commitments are quickly forgotten, and I thrill with anticipation for the adventure that lies ahead.

A bulrush stem scrapes the passing hull, and the sudden noise causes a nearby pied-billed grebe to dive. When the grey bird resurfaces, the "periscope up" silhouette of its head and neck confirms its identity.

Grebes in a marsh are like chickadees in a woodlot—the place just wouldn't be the same without them. These dumpy little birds, outfitted with what appear to be undersized wings, their legs attached seemingly too far back on their bodies, survive quite well in marshlands.

Grebes build floating nests, which they moor to a clump of bulrushes or some dead twig, and use solar energy to help incubate their eggs. In the morning they drape wet vegetation over the eggs. As it dries during the day, the warm sunlight heats the nest. At night, the female grebe pushes aside the now-dry plant material and takes over until dawn.

Pied-billed grebes, so-called for the black ring around their yellow-white beaks, also go by the name

When canoeing through a marsh or beaver pond, look for the leaves and blooms of watershield. This plant is a favourite food of the moose. The large mammals will wade in almost over their heads to get at the succulent stems and roots. The stems are attached at the centre of the floating leaves, making them easy to identify.

FACING PAGE: Green herons appear unconcerned about being seen. They boldly nest above hardwood trees, sometimes a considerable distance from the marsh, and fly back and forth between nest and feeding area.

On patrol over any wet area, gulls, such as this herring gull, are sharp-eyed scavengers. Dead fish, litter, hatching turtles, and unguarded eggs are all acceptable fare to these birds.

Gulls locate their nests on offshore islands in nearby lakes, and usually use wetlands as resting and feeding areas.

of water-witch. This moniker comes from the birds' ability to dive and resurface elsewhere quickly and quietly.

Easing the canoe into a small bay sheltered by cattails, I come across a roost of tree swallows, hundreds of them, perched on the bent green stalks. Although summer still has several weeks left, the birds are already staging for their flight south. Some note the presence of canoe and paddler but are still too chilled from the night to take flight. Others keep their heads tucked down to retain what body heat they have. My intrusion has awakened many, but since the sun has now broken away from the horizon, it is time they were up, anyway.

With twisting, pulling strokes, I back-paddle out of the cove and move on.

Overhead, gulls are flying in loose formation as they leave a nearby lake to feed inland on the beetle larva and worms that abound in the freshly plowed fields. The marsh seems strangely empty of these birds, which just a few months earlier were quite common here.

The reason for their profusion then was the annual spring break-up. The countless dead minnows, catfish, and insects uncovered by the disappearing ice made this area a major feeding site for both gulls and crows. Few of these birds visit the marsh after the ice is gone, since food can be more easily obtained behind tractor and plow than in the deep, sheltered waters of the marsh.

A quick movement within the dense foliage catches my eye, and I flatten the paddle in the water to slow the canoe. When the canoe finally stops, I investigate the vegetation to see what moved. A bird? Or was it just a wayward leaf springing back? In a world where movement reveals presence, movement must be investigated.

A glint of sunlight exposes a beak and a watchful eye. Standing as though carved from wood and placed on a floating rootstalk, an American bittern gazes balefully at me. Despite the noise I've made, the bittern hasn't moved a fraction. The vertical stripes of this bird's plumage match the vertical plane of the cattail leaves surrounding it. This cryptic camouflage of light and dark stripes works equally well for capturing prey or avoiding predators.

Swallows and terns are now skimming the marsh

Floating jauntily on the water is the aquatic smartweed, a food plant for many animals.

The muskrat lodge is an example of how a species can make full use of its environment. After the roots of cattails, bulrushes, and water lily are dug up for food, the leftover leaves are used to build a lodge. Similar to beaver lodges in shape, but smaller and totally organic, muskrat lodges are usually located in the middle of a clearing. As mud and roots are pushed up onto the lodges, small ponds are created, allowing ducks to land, insects to hunt and be hunted, and sunlight to penetrate these new areas. In short, a mini-ecosystem is sustained within the home territory of a muskrat.

Hidden within the jungle of cattail stems and leaves, the American bittern is almost impossible to observe. When in danger, it points its beak upward and freezes in position, masterfully blending with the surrounding vegetation. This young one, just out of its nest, still sports down on the tips of its growing feathers.

ABOVE AND FACING PAGE: Moorhens are probably much more plentiful in wetlands than is commonly thought, but their secretive ways make them difficult to spot. When they feed in the early morning they are bolder, but scoot back to the sheltering cattails at the first sign of trouble.

surface, collecting a well-balanced breakfast of dragonflies, minnows, mosquitoes, and water. As the canoe approaches, small groups of ducklings quickly follow their mothers to hiding places.

Cutting across the quiet surface is a bright-eyed, bewhiskered creature with a long rudderlike tail. It is a muskrat on patrol, come to investigate who is trespassing on his territory.

Muskrats are perhaps the most important mammals a marsh can have, as they keep the prolific cattail growth under control. They eat the roots and leaves, dig channels through the roots, and employ all parts of the plant as building material for their lodges. Without the muskrat constantly putting pressure on the cattails, this marsh vegetation would grow so thick that water-loving creatures would be forced to search for new open-water areas.

A sudden splash from behind me is immediately answered by a trumpetlike call beside me. Holding my breath, I wait to see if the moorhens will emerge through the thick screen of green. Eventually they do—a hen and three young ones, picking their way along a partially submerged log.

The adult bird circles her young, her brilliant red beak and forehead flashing in the sunlight. The youngsters, fuzzy with dull greenish-grey feathers, cavort awkwardly, dashing past one another as they try to snatch the next damselfly. Witnessing some of the daily activities of wildlife is always a special privilege.

The Earth has now rotated just enough for the sun to throw its warm rays over the tips of the cattails and canary grasses, and the stronger light reminds me that I should return to the dock since I need to be on my way to work.

This early-morning trek covered only one hundred metres—no need to travel great distances to find life in a wetland, for life is everywhere, much of it easily seen. This paddle took a mere half-hour, but has given me memories that will last a lifetime.

Dragons in the Air

The morning dew hangs heavy on grasses alongside the trail I am following and has soaked through my worn leather boots. The trail winds around the marsh, sometimes skirting the new growth of cattails, other times plunging through thickets of dogwood and alder.

This June morning the ubiquitous red-winged blackbirds are particularly busy, and for good reason—their eggs have been hatching the past few days. With four pink-and-yellow mouths to feed in each nest, the parent birds are kept gainfully employed finding enough food to fill the gaping beaks.

Both parents will bring home such delicacies as caterpillars, worms, dragonflies, butterflies, and beetle larvae, but the female is the one who will do the bulk of the work. The male, with his familiar red shoulder patches, fancies himself better suited to defending his territory than foraging for his offspring. And he has a point. An undefended area means free pickings for the neighbours, who are only too happy to take food wherever it's easiest to find.

Suddenly all around me the air shimmers with what looks like bits of cellophane! Fluttering up from the tall grasses are thousands of dragonflies. Having spent their youth underwater as fierce predators, these insects are now forsaking their aquatic world to become aerial specialists.

Kneeling, I part the thick tufts of grasses that grow in the wet soil alongside the trail and find the trashy remains of larval dragonflies littering the ground. Once again a cycle of life has been completed in the marsh. Two years earlier a pair of dragonflies mated and the female laid her eggs. She does this by landing on a plant stem rising from the water, dipping her abdomen below the calm surface, and attaching her eggs to the plant's stalk.

When the eggs hatched, the young nymphs scuttled down the stem to the concealing silt of the marsh bottom, where they lived for at least one summer, searching for other insects to eat and hiding from the fish that threatened to eat them.

The nymphs are always a dull greenish-brown, the same colour as the rotting debris amid which they live. In fact, most of the creatures inhabiting the marsh bottom have the same colouring, making the hunt for food all the more difficult.

Dragonfly nymphs share their watery living space with many bizarre-looking animals. Water scorpions have strawlike breathing tubes attached to their back ends, and viselike grabbing forelegs in front;

Having just crawled out from its larval case, where it has spent the past two years, a new dragonfly waits for its wings to dry and strengthen. Because dragonflies are easy prey during this part of their metamorphosis, they hide in the tall grasses that border the marsh.

FACING PAGE: When the time is right, dragonfly nymphs leave the water in a mass exodus, with most of the hatch occurring within forty-eight hours. Thousands of dragonflies will moult their exoskeletons and emerge as flying, insect-eating adults. These dragonflies will track and capture many mosquitoes and flies before hungry birds nab the dragonflies in turn.

Another species with an unmistakable emergence is the mayfly. This insect usually lives as a larva along the shores of lakes and appears in springtime by the millions. Fish and birds devour most mayflies before they live out their short two-day lives as winged adults.

Life is often violent below the surface of the water, and one of the most ferocious predators is the giant water bug. It waits quietly in ambush for a minnow, tadpole, or dragonfly nymph to come by, then lashes out with powerful forelegs to capture its meal.

A living, deadly snorkel, the water scorpion waits with tail tube poised above the surface of the water. Like the giant water bug, this creature captures unwary passers-by with its hooked forelegs, then stabs its hypodermic mouth part into its victim's body and sucks it dry.

and giant water bugs, whose huge, all-seeing eyes and strong pincers make life hectic for anything within striking range. Neither of these bugs has jaws, just a hollow, needlelike mouth part, which they stab into their prey to suck out body fluids.

Diving beetles, which carry air bubbles under their wings while submerged, scoot about looking for careless damsel-fly nymphs. And there are whirligig beetles, with two sets of eyes, one to search prey below the surface of the water, the other to observe approaching predators above the surface.

The dragonflies are among the more voracious members of the underwater community and they grow quickly. As they grow they shed their skin, or moult, several times. Actually, their outer layer is not really "skin," but exoskeleton, the hard surface that holds the young dragonfly together. After their final moult they will leave their familiar home, never to return.

Overnight, the nymphs crawl out of the water and up the first bit of substantial vegetation they encounter. Throughout the night their exoskeletons split and they shed the confining casings the way we might take off a sweater. At first their wings are damp and crumpled, but they begin to unfurl as their bodies pump fluids into the transparent appendages. As the morning sun reaches them the wings dry and harden to perfection.

When the ambient air temperature reaches that magic level of warmth where insects can fly easily, the newly emerged dragonflies take flight, heading in all directions at once. Thin, membranous wings carry the dark-bodied insects aloft on invisible microthermals. Rising, then dropping, skittering sideways, banking, diving, the dragonflies disperse in search of food and mates.

Dragonflies are wonderfully adapted flying hunters. Their large compound eyes catch even subtle movements of other insects, and their gossamer wings propel them with enough force to overtake almost any insect that dares to fly close by.

Once a dragonfly gets a bead on a mosquito or fly, it traps it in midair within a bristly basket formed by holding its legs together. Dragonflies often consume their prey while flying, shooting out their unique lower mandibles and pulling the captured insect into their mouths.

The dragonflies had just begun their maiden flights as I came upon them, legions of them lifting into the air almost en masse, displaying no apprehension about leaving behind the safety of the water. Now most have disappeared from view. Either they are perching on twigs overhead or have set a course that will take them out over the stands of cattails.

I am about to continue my walk, when a cluster of glistening droplets near the top of a tall grassy

Still blind, these baby red-winged black-birds wait for their mother to return with food. Whenever I simulated the arrival of an adult bird by jiggling their nest, four pink-and-yellow beaks shot up in anticipation of a juicy morsel.

stem catches my eye. Looking closer, I make a most wonderful discovery. It is a lone dragonfly which has become enshrouded in dewdrops while resting for the night. This early morning spectacle of sunlight playing through the dew on the dragonfly's membranous wings, creating a rainbow of colours, is dazzling, and I am struck with awe, so beautiful is the sight. An illustrator depicting a fairy princess on her wedding day would have difficulty equaling the delicate beauty of this natural phenomenon.

A breeze arrives with the rising temperature, and I resume my hike, one dragonfly resting on my hat, two more on my jacket, and another wondrous event of nature tucked away in my memory.

Sunset

Sunset brings a certain restlessness to the marsh, a quiet excitement as the sun slips away. This is when a "changing of the guard" takes place, and species that slumbered during the day eagerly begin their search for food, while those sated from their foraging anxiously seek shelter before the nocturnal predators emerge.

Overhead fly ragged flocks of ducks, on their way from the wetland to forage for their supper in nearby fields. These are young birds: just one season earlier they had not even hatched. Now they leave their parents behind, flightless in their moults. The adult drakes and hens hide in the thick stands of cattails and bulrushes, waiting for new feathers to grow so that they can join their progeny in the air.

In the marsh's calm water two young pied-billed grebes chase after their mother, anticipating the tasty small fish in her beak. She teases her offspring as a way of training the youngsters to fight for their food. This, however, is a skill they will acquire with agonizing slowness. Across the open sections of the marsh four more families of grebes are learning the same lesson.

The marsh water has taken on a warm glow, reflecting the last of the day's sunlight. Although it is becoming difficult to see, black terns continue to fish. Swirling, skimming, fluttering, they patrol the marsh for minnows and large insects. A swoop, a tiny ripple, and they pluck a hapless fish from the still waters.

Unlike baby grebes, young terns are doted upon by their parents. They sit on weathered stumps and chirp at the passing adults until one hovers at their head and drops some still-wriggling supper into their mouths. Impatient at times, the young terns take flight and chase the adults, encouraging them to catch more, and more again.

At twilight, when the sun has dropped below the horizon yet still lights the sky with its amazing power, the marsh world loses colour and all things take on shades of grey. Silhouettes fly by, and identifying the marsh denizens becomes a challenge.

A startling rush of wings marks the arrival of many red-winged blackbirds—the first flock returning to the marsh to roost for the night. Another flock appears in the darkening haze, then another. The birds are noisy and restless, still eager to feed. They are mainly females and young ones; the males congregate in their own flocks and will be the last to arrive at night.

Dead trees standing stark and bare a moment ago are bedecked with blackbirds, and once more

FACING PAGE: As the sun disappears for the night, young Canada geese forage in the aquatic growth.

The serenity of a wetland.

*Words cannot capture the beauty of a
marsh at sunset or even begin to
describe the emotions you feel. Only
those who have been there can know how
good the experience is for the soul.*

Canary grass, also known as phragmites, is an artistically pleasing wetland species, no matter how you look at it. Like cattails and bulrushes, canary grass is synonymous with marshland, and an integral part of a complex community.

During late summer the blackbirds begin to stage in preparation for their fall migration. Territorial boundaries are forgotten, families intermingle, and the flocks grow in size to comprise hundreds of thousands of birds. The birds find food and roosting sites within the larger marshes, "refoliating" dead trees with their presence.

appear thick with foliage. By early September thousands upon thousands of red-winged blackbirds will seek nightly refuge on them in the marsh.

Sharing the treetop roosts are hunch-shouldered, long-legged herons. Three species will be here tonight, but only one will be active. While the great blue herons and green-backed herons rest with heads tucked under their wings, the black-crowned night herons will seek food in the wetland below.

With their striking black, silver, and white plumage, which blends with the shadows and moonlit reflections of the marsh, night herons appear made for evening foraging. When the dusk thickens, the barking calls of these birds intensify as they set out for a night's hunt.

Now the young ducks return. Flying silent and low, these brothers and sisters have had their fill of grain and weed seeds and are coming home for the night. They land with little fanfare in the far reaches of the marsh. Their crops are full and they don't want to attract the attention of great horned owls or raccoons.

Throughout the evening, people too have been drawn to the marsh. A father and son share photography equipment; a young couple with their new baby sit by the shore; a group of boys, dip nets bristling, excitedly fill a pail with their finds; a small group of mothers walk the marsh edge with their daughters. We do not know one another, yet we smile and exchange pleasantries as we pass.

The marsh is not on a main tourist route, so getting here is difficult. Yet the rewards for making the effort are great. From the leopard frog that hops between our feet to the great blue heron that flies up at our approach, from the familiar ducks overhead to the strange, exotic calls from within the cattail jungle, bountiful nature surrounds us and we are awed.

At last it is dark. A faint afterglow outlines the western horizon as the stars begin to twinkle in the heavens. Those of us who have shared the coming of evening have had a feast—not one to sustain the body, but one for the heart and soul.

Wetlands are wonderful places!

Just as the sun drops to the western horizon, the ducks come back to the marsh from their evening feed in the nearby fields. The geese will return a half-hour later, gliding in as black silhouettes to settle for the night.

Winter

It always amazes me how fast the marsh can change its look, its inhabitants, indeed its entire character. A few days earlier I would have needed a canoe to get where I am now, but three days and nights of calm, deadly cold have neatly sealed the water. The ice is already thick enough to support me, and I shuffle and slide cautiously, awkwardly, across the smooth surface to explore a winter wetland.

My shadow mutes the sun's glare, allowing me a unique view through the clear ice. I kneel to peer through this magical looking-glass at the world below, and my stomach tenses at the eerie sensation I have of being suspended.

I see no schools of fish flashing by, no lumbering snapping turtles, not even a wiggling insect. All is still, as if this world were a masterfully set up aquarium still awaiting occupants. Yet life is there.

Millions, perhaps billions, of eggs are attached to the decaying vegetation. Deposited mainly by insects, either in clusters or singly, the leathery containers are full of life. For now they are content to wait in the chilly four-degree Celsius water, but once the warmth of spring returns, the eggs will burst open with a new generation. The adults that produced this next generation are dead, having succumbed to predators, the cold, or lack of oxygen.

While the marsh slumbers, death waits patiently. The lid of ice acts as a barrier between the oxygen-rich air and the oxygen-dependent life forms in the water. In spring, summer, and fall oxygen is added to the water through wave action, rainfall, and when the growing vegetation releases it as a gas during photosynthesis. Soon the thickening layers of snow will completely block the light. When the light disappears, the plants cease growing, shutting down the only underwater source of oxygen available!

In early spring the bodies of fish and invertebrates such as backswimmers and water boatmen will pile up along the shoreline—testimony that the months-long struggle for life is sometimes in vain. No wonder the surviving animals show great joy in springtime, for the frugalities of winter living can then be relegated to memory.

Surrounding the natural rink are the tattered and sun-bleached leaves of last year's cattails. The puffy seed heads are scattered throughout the marsh, some still packed tight in the familiar "hot dog on a

Black-capped chickadees tear apart cattail heads, not to eat the tiny seeds but to find the larvae of the cattail moth, which overwinters in the heads. The fluff will be used as nest material later in the spring.

FACING PAGE: The first ice of the season is always a shock—suddenly winter is really here. But the shock is softened by the beauty of the thin ice.

*This ice formation is the result of warm
weather. Snow melted and dripped onto
the ice, while at the same time the stream
rose and fell with fluctuating snowmelt.
Like dipping candles, the icicles grew
fatter with each passing wave.*

A vivid imagination helps when interpreting ice formations. Here we see a surrealistic Inuit spirit, or the cosmos, or....

During spring break-up, gulls and crows gather to feast on the bounty of minnows and insects killed by the winter cold. Without this clean-up crew, the marsh would be a fetid place once the water warms up.

stick" shape of summer. Most have burst open, though, their almost microscopic seeds spread by the bitter winds that catch the tiny parachutes.

Within the well-insulated seed heads live the larvae of the cattail moth, trying to survive the frigid season. But the chickadees have learned of their presence, and take great delight in tearing open the woolly seedheads to have a high-protein snack.

Despite the inhospitable look of the winter cattails, several species of wildlife seek shelter within them. Pheasants hide from owls, mice elude mink, and European hare (jackrabbits) escape the weather.

A lost gust of wind dances through the cattails and the resulting raspy rattle gives fair warning to heavier creatures to keep away. The torn leaves hold the gentle snowflakes above the water, and in time will support the entire winter's blanket of snow. But since snow insulates, the water below does not become cool enough to freeze, or freeze substantially enough to support much weight. Many snowmobilers who have disregarded these waving remnants of summer have gone for a midwinter swim.

Within this no-man's-land of ivory cattail leaves sit a cluster of dark mounds on the ice. They are the cozy winter homes of the muskrats, one of the most common inhabitants of a marsh. These piles of mud mixed with plant stems and roots were built in late fall with such speed that they appeared to materialize overnight.

Coyotes often venture onto the ice in the hope of digging into these warm homes and securing a meal for the day. Great horned and snowy owls also keep an eye on the dark mounds in case a resident decides to surface for an hour of sunbathing.

While some muskrats die by fang or talon, others simply succumb to the emotionless cold. Winds whip through every exposed crack in the lodges, and occasionally an individual perishes because of a poorly constructed home.

Winter should be a time of quiet rest, yet for the inhabitants of the marsh, it is a time of hardship, fear, and death.

The cold winds blow harder now and cause the spirits of the marsh to begin their singing. Every crack, crevice, and hole in the nearby dead trees begins to hum and howl as the wind rushes by. This symphony of mournful cries is a sad, winter sound, and I am glad to be on my way again, soon to be sheltered within a warm building from the winter's harsh cold.

Drifting snow catches on marsh vegetation and creates hummocks on the flat ice. These will collect more snow each time the winds blow. Because the interlocking snowflakes insulate, the air trapped below the snow may actually reach thawing temperatures and soften the ice in spots.

SWAMPS AND BEAVER PONDS

What Value Is a Swamp?

Anyone who wants to experience the countryside as it was before development invaded should wade into one of the few remaining older swamps.

As you enter a swamp the interwoven greenery of leaves, vines, mosses, and lichens envelops you, and the thick foliage makes even the simple act of walking a challenge. Keeping track of your bearings borders on the impossible. But as you recognize the lady's-slipper orchids and other wildflowers, and identify the songs of the ovenbird and hermit thrush, you begin to feel more at ease—and quite intrigued.

A fallen log, covered with moss, liverworts, lichens, and mushrooms, becomes an outdoor classroom, a lesson in symbiotic relationships, food chains and food webs, decomposers, and opportunists. The log is a micro-world of organisms that interact in an orderly fashion, each playing a role that both depends on and supports the other players.

Although it hasn't rained for several days, your boots are soaked from the water held in the ground cover. Gently pull a handful of moss loose, then squeeze it, and nearly a handful of water is released. Several million litres of water are held, drop by drop, within this thick green mat. The damp, black soil below retains even more of this precious liquid.

As these unassuming ground-cover plants grow, nourished by the moisture they have trapped, they give off a waste product—oxygen. In terms of oxygen production and energy conversion, wetlands are almost equal to similar-sized areas of rain forest. Changing pure sunlight into viable biomass (the physical, three-dimensional food and shelter required by living species) is a marvelous feat of nature. Only plants can do this, and wetlands are home to the greatest number of plants found in any habitat.

When asked to name some types of wetland wildlife, the species that usually come to mind are beaver, muskrat, turtles, fish, ducks and geese. While these species are certainly among the more common ones that live in

FACING PAGE: The cool, rich, wet, slightly acidic organic soils of the swamp provide the necessary ingredients for orchids to thrive. Yellow and showy lady's-slipper orchids are among the most easily seen; several more species, smaller and less conspicuous, hide amid the green mosses of this wetland.

Have you heard the bullfrogs calling lately? Probably not. Their deep jug-o-rum cries have disappeared from many places because of pond drainage, pollution, acid rain, and, in some areas, market hunting for frogs' legs. Distinguishable from green frogs by their larger size, the shape of their foot, and the ridge of folded skin around their eardrums (tympana), bullfrogs are a special find.

The solitude, isolation, and dead trees of a large swamp are ideal for establishing a heronry. Great blue herons, great egrets, night herons, and green herons do not like their nests disturbed; where better to place them than the centre of a swamp?

Swamps and beaver ponds are practically synonymous, since each is usually the result of the other. Newly flooded forests will drown many trees, but water-tolerant tree species will thrive. This blend of open water and protective vegetation is very attractive to wildlife.

The leaves of the jewelweed (also called touch-me-not) are covered with microscopic hairs that repel water, causing dew and rain to bead on the surface. Hold a leaf underwater—in a beam of sunlight it will appear to be made of tin foil—then remove it, and it will be perfectly dry. The ripened seed pods of jewelweed "explode" when brushed by passing animals, throwing the seeds a metre or more. On some people the sap of this plant cures a poison ivy rash.

a wetland, many other forms of wildlife also depend on wetlands for their survival.

The water held in a swamp is what makes the swamp so valuable. This was illustrated to me one day as three deer—a doe and two fawns—stood in open view at the edge of a swamp, the low angle of the early morning sun spotlighting them against the dark greens of the thick woodland foliage. While the youngsters took turns dropping their heads to sip the clear water, the doe kept a constant watch, her twitching ears, piercing eyes, and inquisitive nose making sure I didn't get any closer.

Not only do deer require water daily, so do all the other woodland creatures, such as raccoons, squirrels, porcupines, crows, and ruffed grouse.

Of course I had always known that they needed water, but hadn't really thought about where this water comes from. Some moisture certainly reaches animals as rain, dew, or snow. But if not for a constant, dependable source, such as a swamp, they could not survive, and the surrounding forest would be the poorer in both variety and abundance of life.

Even the trees themselves, which offer food and shelter to so many creatures, could not survive if this water table disappeared, or was altered. Over the centuries this woodlot was created because of the water held within the soil. Red maple, ash, and balsam fir, the predominant tree species in swamps, all require abundant moisture for their root systems.

When swamps are drained, the tree roots dry out and thus die. When a tree dies, its leaves, which provide food and cover for wildlife, are the first thing to go. Without a thick canopy of leaves to shade and cool the forest floor, the drying-out process is accelerated, and soon all manner of life suffers.

The water within a wetland such as a swamp is more than just a home for ducks, beavers, and fish. It is the lifeblood of a vast range of flora and fauna.

Humans are not excluded from this intricate web of relationships. Like the woodland deer, we, too, require fresh, clean water during all seasons of the year. And that water comes from our few remaining swamps and marshes. Water that begins as rain or snow is held and filtered within the swamps and

Wetlands provide life to more than just wetland species. White-tailed deer are just one example. Wetlands are nature's reservoirs, temporarily holding and slowly releasing the collected snowmelt and rainwater, thereby ensuring life for all species.

Rarely can you find a plant that actually thrives on pollution, but wild calla is one. Content to grow in freshwater ponds and along stream banks, it also does well in seepage areas. This photo was taken at the local dump, a landfill situated on top of a swamp and beside a lake. The trapped water was fetid yet a half-hectare of land was covered in this beautiful wildflower.

FACING PAGE: The shade and wetness of the forest floor of a swamp determine what can grow there. The ground cover may be sphagnum moss, a succulent plant that holds incredible amounts of water. This characteristic was used to advantage by natives and settlers, who employed sphagnum moss as chinking between the logs of cabins and as diapers for their papooses (the first disposable diaper!). Today the plant is used by some manufacturers as part of sanitary napkins.

marshes before it eventually makes its way into our wells, aquifers, and pumps.

Swamps are a part of our natural history and our social history. They are special places that are under siege, and have been so for quite some time. Perhaps this is because many people still look upon swamps as dismal places to be avoided, places full of unknown diseases and threatening creatures.

These notions are wrong. They are ideas left over from the era of settlement, when wet areas were by-passed in favour of the unending forests and the fertile soils found beneath them. The less fortunate settlers obtained property that included large wet areas, and since water always flows downhill, their attempts at clearing the land were usually futile. Thus was born the idea that wetlands were wastelands, places to be shunned and scorned or drained and conquered.

The Industrial Age brought great advancements in farming techniques. Pumps, backhoes, culverts, and tile drains gave farmers and, later, land developers, a formidable arsenal with which to attack the dreaded swamps.

Yet, in reality, wetlands are the most productive type of habitat anyone could wish for. Their value to our economy and our lifestyles is inestimable. Nevertheless, we still drain, fill, and pollute them, with little concern.

All those pockets of water act as reservoirs, filters, erosion-control sites, and sediment-deposition areas. The wetlands that have been spared from "development" dutifully continue to fulfill these functions and supply us with a wonderful range of life. When will we realize that these wetland complexes are of great value to wildlife and people alike?

Even though we'll never again see the vast swamps and marshes that existed as recently as sixty years ago, we can still explore the remnants of these unappreciated sites, and with camera and notebook record the beauty that remains.

Spring Walk

Just as red-winged blackbirds occupy marshes, common grackles live in the swamps. Their grating calls echo through the dead trees as they find and claim hollows and stake out their territories. Grackles eat insects, and the abundance of aquatic species ensures easy pickings.

The sun blinds me as I step outside, but the warm breeze that caresses my face makes up for the shock. While I wait for my eyes to adjust to the brightness, my ears pick up a number of spring sounds. Grackles, hundreds of them, are calling from the dead trees that surround the marsh. The grating, squeaking cries of these large blackbirds are actually quite musical when heard as an ensemble.

I set off toward a nearby swamp to look for signs of spring: birds that have arrived, shoots pushing up through the rotting leaves, buds bursting open to celebrate winter's demise. The woods are free of snow now, and the layer of wet leaves pads my footsteps. Nevertheless, silence alone isn't enough for me to sneak up on some creatures.

A flock of wood ducks sitting in a meltwater pond have already noted my presence. I didn't see them until they burst into the air, their shrill calls of *who-eek! who-eek!* echoing off the leafless trees. The colouration of the males is absolutely stunning in springtime.

No doubt female wood ducks are nearby, searching for a suitable site to lay their eggs. Unlike many other species of ducks, woodies nest inside hollow trees. When the ducklings leave the nest, their first challenge in life is to survive the several-metre fall from the nest entrance to the ground!

A unique world of life exists in these ephemeral ponds of melted snow. Eggs from grey tree frogs, wood frogs, salamanders, and mosquitoes abound. Aquatic insects, some associated with more permanent bodies of water, also live here, foraging for food wherever they can find it.

One of the miracles of nature appears here, the beautiful, elusive fairy shrimp. Their bodies are translucent, tinged with a light orange colour, and tiny—no longer than a third of your finger. Fairy shrimp hide with ease in the submerged, rotting leaves of autumn past. In the short time the pond exists, these shrimp hatch, mate, lay eggs, and die.

Their eggs are the size of dust particles, and are attached to the underside of the waterlogged leaves of maple and poplar. By early summer these pockets of water will no longer exist—evaporated by the warming sun and the gentle breezes. The leaves dry and curl, and the swirling air picks them up and moves them along the forest floor, depositing them in another depression downwind. The eggs of the

FACING PAGE: This young Midland painted turtle was an egg about one year ago. Adult females leave the wetlands to lay their eggs in June; the eggs incubate in the underground nest for several months, then hatch in autumn; the hatchlings may leave the nest at that time, or opt to stay put for the winter and make the dash for water next spring.

This female snapping turtle has dug her nest and is now depositing a dozen eggs the size of table-tennis balls. When finished, she will cover the white eggs with dirt, then return to the sanctuary of the swamp. The sex of the hatchlings is determined by the temperature at which the eggs incubate: below sixty-eight degrees Fahrenheit and they will be males, above this and they will be females.

fairy shrimp hitch a ride to wherever, and wait through summer's heat and winter's cold before hatching the following spring.

Nearby, the churring rattle of a kingfisher sounds. As soon as the ice opens enough for the birds to spot minnows from the air, the kingfishers arrive. One flies past—a male, since it lacks the brown belly band found on females.

Crossing an old beaver dam, which still cannot stem the flow of snowmelt, I notice dark shadows on the bottom of the stream. Those shadows weren't there yesterday, and as I watch, they are no longer where they were just a moment ago.

A quick flash of cream-coloured belly explains the phenomenon—the northern pike are spawning! Swimming upstream from the open waters of the bay, these fish return to the swamps each year to lay their eggs. The sluggish females are escorted by smaller, darting males as the cycle of life begins anew. Some streams attract pickerel; others draw rainbow trout. The wetlands, which are the headwaters of these waterways, become nurseries for the young fish, places to grow before they must face the perils of deep water.

A small voice calls from a swampy area beside a flooded field. Small, but loud. For when a spring peeper goes looking for a mate, the whole countryside knows about it. Another joins him, then another, and soon the damp spring air rings with a sleigh-bell chorus of frogs.

Only a handful of wildlife calls can still raise the small hairs on the backs of our necks or cause our hearts to beat faster: the howl of a wolf, the yodel of a loon, the call of a Canada goose—and the chorus of these tiny tree frogs. These calls are the epitome of wilderness, cathartic for a dulled spirit. They enter our ears, reverberate within our chests, and settle into our souls. They are good sounds.

An opening in the thick band of shrubs that borders the swamp reveals a large flooded area. Most of the ice has disappeared and each patch of open water now hosts a flock of ducks.

You hardly need colour film to photograph these species, since black-and-white is the dress code for the diving ducks. Ring-necked ducks, goldeneyes, buffleheads, lesser scaups, and common mergansers share the waters with ring-billed and herring gulls. Crows line the edges of the icy openings, searching for dead minnows.

If you spend much time in the out of doors, you will probably have occasion to witness at least one unusual event. It may be something that occurs regularly but is seldom seen—a deer giving birth—or it may be a special view of something rare—perhaps a peregrine falcon landing on the tree in front of you. Or it may be a chance encounter between species that normally do not interact—a kitten and a groundhog rubbing noses, for example.

A few weeks after this first spring outing, I witnessed a common, yet seldom seen, event. It hap-

The spring-flooded swamps and marshes of the lower Great Lakes region are the nurseries for many species of fish. Northern pike come upstream in early April to lay their eggs, as do pickerel. The adult fish must then escape downstream to larger lakes before water levels drop, trapping them behind beaver dams.

It's hard to imagine how the brightly plumed wood duck could possibly escape the notice of its predators. Yet the bird's bold colours and striking pattern allow it to camouflage quite well within the shrubby growth of a swamp. The wood duck's alert nature also makes it difficult for predators to approach it closely.

The first ducks to arrive in the spring are usually the divers, the birds of the northern lakes. Dressed formally in black-and-white, ring-necked ducks and hooded mergansers drop into beaver swamps and open ditches, seeking a meal of minnows and small crustaceans.

Some frogs live year-round in a swamp; others use it for only part of their life cycle. Grey tree frogs and American toads hibernate beneath the frozen waters, as do spring peepers. As soon as the ice turns to water, the frogs and toads emerge and begin trilling to attract a mate.

Once the eggs have been deposited in the shallow waters, the adults depart from the swamp. Toads travel to fields and gardens, while tree frogs climb upward to live an arboreal life for the summer. The peepers will remain in the swamp, but seldom call after their breeding season.

pened where the hard-packed nature trail turned from wetland into field, where the underlying soil changed from black organic to hard clay.

Lying across the pathway was a twig about the diameter of a pencil, over which a small, muddy disk first teetered, then fell. I looked more closely and saw four legs and a head jutting out from the quarter-sized disc.

It was a baby painted turtle, which had just emerged from its nest. A second, then a third turtle materialized, pint-sized replicas of their parents. A fourth suddenly appeared, as if spit out of the earth itself. What I was seeing was the emergence of a nest of turtles that had survived predators, frost, and drought.

Almost a year earlier, a female painted turtle had left the swamp under cover of darkness, climbed the steep and heavily vegetated embankment, and dug a vase-shaped hole in the clay. She laid eight eggs, covered them and smoothed the soil, then returned to the nearby protective waters of the swamp.

Perhaps because the nest sat right on the walkway, human scent masked the odour of the eggs, thereby depriving raccoons and skunks of another easy meal (most turtle nests are doomed to be preyed upon by these two scavengers). The sun incubated the eggs all summer and in October the new turtles hatched.

But even though they had broken free of their eggshells, they didn't leave the underground nest. Instead they opted to overwinter there, huddled together to survive the freezing temperatures and living off a yolk sac while the ground around them turned to the consistency of rock. This ability to survive adverse conditions is just one of the many ways turtles are remarkable animals.

On this warm spring day they appear to have decided unanimously that it was the right day to emerge! After digging a narrow tunnel to the surface, out they came, each blinking in the bright sunlight.

Covered with dried clay, only their eyes appearing damp, they set out purposefully, each taking a route unto himself.

If they can avoid gulls, crows, snakes, raccoons, mink, skunks, herons, cars, and curious children, they will live for about fifteen years. The females will not be able to lay eggs during the first five years of their lives, for it takes that long for them to mature.

Once the females reach breeding age, they will leave the wetland on a warm June night, climb up this same embankment, and, acting on instincts eons old, dig shallow nests in the hardened ground. They will deposit their eggs and slip away before sunrise.

And maybe, just maybe, when those hatchlings emerge from their earthen womb a year later, there will again be someone passing by who will witness, enjoy, and learn from this annual miracle of nature.

Swamp Stop

Five o'clock and I'm out the door, heading for home. But along the way I'll stop at a favourite watering hole, a place where I can unwind from the tensions of the day—a quiet roadside swamp!

This fondness for swamps dates back to childhood. My earliest lessons in limnology, the study of freshwater life, were in a cow pond on my uncle's farm. Of course, my cousins and I had no idea at the time that what we were doing was called limnology; we didn't even realize that what we were doing was educational. We were just having fun "muckin' about in the swamp."

Throughout those wonderful summers, we got to know every mossy log, dark hole, hidden nest, and shy inhabitant of that unassuming wet patch in the field. With collecting equipment that consisted of a couple of preserving jars and a wire sieve, liberated with great stealth from my aunt's kitchen, we became adventurers and biologists simply because of what nature provided for us.

And what a bounty of life there was to explore! Tadpoles, water scorpions, newts, green frogs, caddis flies, and kingfishers became the subjects of our investigations. We imprisoned frogs' eggs or backswimmers in a glass sealer and left them there for about three minutes before dumping them unceremoniously back into the pond, to make way for a newly caught stickleback or whirligig beetle!

Now, as the road drops over a knoll and through a treed swamp, I roll down the window, let up on the gas pedal, and steer the car onto the gravel shoulder; I am eager to experience that world again.

Even before the car stops rolling, a pair of mallard ducks leaps from the water and takes flight. They circle the area once, the hen quacking loudly, the drake following dutifully behind, then set their wings to drift down into the heavy vegetation at the far side of the swamp.

I remain in the car but poke my head and shoulders out the open window. The air is so refreshing, clean, with the scent of wildflowers on it. Wild iris and both white and yellow water lilies abound, creating a wonderfully fragrant bouquet.

Nearby, the calm surface of the pewter-coloured water is silently torn by a muskrat returning home with a mouthful of new-growth cattail. It pauses and does a good imitation of a floating log, suddenly aware that the isolated world of the swamp isn't quite so isolated any more, then dives quickly, leaving

The wild iris appears almost too domestic to be found growing on the scattered hummocks of a swamp. The multicoloured sepals and petals earned this wildflower its name, in honour of the goddess of the rainbow, Iris. The three parts of the blossom are said to represent faith, wisdom, and courage.

FACING PAGE: Just a giant mouse with semi-webbed feet, muskrats are the most common wetland mammals. They produce two litters a year, with an average of six young per litter. When natural mortality and predation are combined with a harvesting program, their population can be maintained at a healthy level.

Testament to a previous habitat, dead trees still provide wildlife with roosts, shelter, and food (wood-boring beetles and carpenter ants, for example, are eaten by woodpeckers).

The fragrant flowers of white water lily adorn most beaver ponds, attracting small wasps and other nectar gatherers. The roots, which have the consistency of a potato, are consumed by beavers, muskrats, moose, and people. The stem attaches to the centre of the leaf so that the leaf cannot twist over in the wind.

Superbly camouflaged, a short-tailed weasel seeks its meal along the shoreline. Small yet feisty, this cousin of the mink is capable of killing cottontail rabbits and adult ducks. It also feeds heavily on mice, voles, frogs, and fish.

a telltale stream of bubbles as it swims to the underwater entrance of its lodge.

Suddenly the air is filled with raucous honking as four Canada geese swing in and land like water-skiers on the open water. They bob their heads and murmur excitedly as they check for other geese. The human visitor is noticed, but the only action they take is to move farther back into a brushy area.

Tree swallows flit low over the pond, cross the roadway, perform aerial acrobatics as they catch the few midges and insects that are about. A car rockets past, the driver seemingly oblivious of me, and certainly of the birds, mammals, and wildflowers living within this roadside swamp. Just as the car flies by, so do the swallows. There is a muffled *thwap* of feathers against steel, and a limp blue-and-white bundle rolls a few feet along the pavement in the vehicle's wake.

Making good use of tree hollows and eating huge quantities of insects every day, tree swallows are very much a part of a swamp ecosystem. Because they are so dependent on flying insects, swallows begin their autumn migration by mid-August, when local insects have become less plentiful.

A shadow rushes by on the pavement. A crow has spotted the dead swallow and arrives for an easy meal. It lands and cocks its head while studying the fluffy morsel. A tentative peck, a head-jerking gulp, and the scruffy beggar departs silently, its role as a scavenger fulfilled.

The sun has slipped low enough to fully light the scene before me. Trees, long dead, still stretch their brittle limbs skyward, providing nest perches and lookouts for blackbirds and swallows. Grackles puff themselves up in self-indulgent importance, squeaking and squealing their grating courtship cries.

The calls and interactions of wildlife, the serene setting, the colourful splashes of blooms, all combine to erase the tensions of the day. It is this aesthetic experience that so many people long for and look forward to with each visit to a wetland.

It's almost dark now, and I get ready to leave. Just as I am about to turn the ignition key, a brown blur catches my eye in the mirror. Hardly a car length behind me, a mink is crossing the road. She pauses only long enough to check both ways for traffic, then bounds across the pavement and into the thick grasses that mark the border of the swamp.

Starting the car draws the attention of the geese, but they don't panic; in fact, they hardly stop feeding. I wait while another car whooshes past; at least its driver looks concerned about *my* presence.

I head off and am almost even with the edge of the wetland when a spring peeper calls once, twice, and then there is silence.

As I drive home I wonder if the little frog was bidding me a farewell or rejoicing that I had finally left the inhabitants of the swamp alone.

Beaver Ponds

FACING PAGE: Located near the centre of the pond, the beaver lodge is well protected from predators. Only the otter can enter the lodge to take the beaver kits. But this is something only a desperate otter will do, since adult beavers can turn into 27 kilograms of fury if provoked.

Spending time at a beaver pond is probably the easiest way to see how nature adapts to change and how species cope with alterations in their habitat, because a beaver pond evolves from forest to swamp to meadow, then back to forest again, and the wildlife and plant communities must adjust to the shift in habitat as best they can.

To have a beaver pond, you first must have a stream that meanders through a forest. Such streams are only a small, visible part of an underground wetland. Even in dry times, water stored in the soil seeps into these troughs, so that the streams continue to flow throughout the summer months.

Trees thrive along the banks of these streams, the species determined by the amount of water that reaches their roots. Very moist soil supports black ash, yellow birch, and red maple; moderate moisture gives life to white birch, sugar maple, and white ash.

Depending on the length of a stream, a series of beaver ponds may be created. As beaver families expand, the youngsters from previous years are sent away to establish their own ponds. Offering both fresh-flowing water and lush vegetation, woodland streams beckon to any beaver searching for a home.

Renowned for their woodworking, beavers come fully equipped for the job with chisel-sharp teeth that gnaw through heavy wood effortlessly. They brace their upper incisors into the log, then bring the lower jaw up with a side to side chewing motion. Once a log is delimbed and cut into manageable lengths, the beavers haul it down to the pond, where they can process it in safety.

Once a pond is created and the flow of water altered, changes in animal life begin immediately. Minnows from the once-fast-flowing current are caught in shallows of the new pond, providing an easy meal to kingfishers, herons, mink, and otters. Some of these predators already patrolled the stream; as the surface of the pond stretches ever wider, others are attracted.

As trees become scarce around the pond's edge, having been used for food and building materials, the beavers must increase the water level to gain access to more distant trees. And so, as the dam grows, the water depth increases and more land is flooded.

This extra water is more than some tree species, such as sugar maple and white ash, can tolerate. If a tree escapes the incisors of a beaver, then it drowns in the new amount of moisture flooding the rootlets. As trees

The crimson blossoms of the cardinal flower are unmistakable and impossible to overlook. As if designed by an advertising agency, this wildflower draws the viewer close because of its colour and shape. Unfortunately, flower pickers have almost decimated this gorgeous wildflower in areas where it was once common.

drown or are cut down, the need for a larger pond continues.

Within a year or two, this flooded area will support a complex wetland community. Certainly the beavers are present, and a few pair of muskrats may also have moved in. Herons feed on the frogs, snakes, and fish in the shallows, and may even nest on top of the dead spirals of drowned cedars and spruce. Wood ducks drop in on each migration, as do ring-necked ducks, hooded mergansers, both blue- and green-winged teals, and a few mallards.

Woodpeckers, nuthatches, chickadees, and brown creepers take advantage of the decaying wood to create homes or search out wood-boring insects for food. The standing, well-rotted stems of white birch are preferred by the black-capped chickadee, while loose bark peeling from dead hardwoods gives the creepers a special place to hide their nests.

The only real threat to a beaver is the otter, a large predatory mammal whose territory includes lakes, bays, streams, and ponds. Otters usually attack the kits while they swim in the pond, but they will also enter the beaver lodge to obtain a meal.

White-tailed deer come to the water's edge to drink, and raccoons forage along the shoreline for snails, crayfish, frogs, and fingernail clams. Mink hunt the stands of cattails and sedges that have sprung up in the nutrient-rich shallows, and if the beaver pond is far enough north, moose may come in the spring to dine on the roots and shoots of the water lily and watershield.

Eventually the beaver eats all the available food and must abandon the pond. Without daily maintenance, the dam soon develops leaks, which quickly turn into major breaks. Wood rots and mud washes away. Before long the pond is gone, leaving an open, meadowlike area with a small stream that follows its original course.

But the thick layer of silt that accumulated behind the dam is rich in nutrients. Moisture-loving grasses, rushes, sedges, and wildflowers quickly claim the sunny, damp site. Purple-fringed orchid, yellow loosestrife, bog goldenrod, New England aster, wild iris, and myriad other species thrive there. In fact, fluctuating water levels are a requirement of some wildflowers.

Honeybees and butterflies are the most obvious users of beaver meadow, but deer also browse in the dim light of dawn and dusk.

Soon a few shoots of dogwood spring up, followed by alder, maple, and ash. As these saplings and shrubs grow, create shade, and drop their leaves, the organic layer changes once again. In a few years,

Stalking the shallows, imitating a weathered tree, a young great blue heron seeks its food. The nest that this bird hatched in may well be at the other end of the pond, clustered with others in the higher branches of the dead trees.

Wherever there is water, there will be raccoons, since food for this scavenger/predator is abundant in the shallows. Frogs, leeches, crayfish, clams, snails, dead fish, and duck eggs give the raccoons a well-balanced diet.

as the rootlets seek out and use the water held in the rich soils, a young forest is produced. And then along comes a beaver.

This cycle has one obvious constant: water. As the wetland changes in the way animals use it and its vegetation, water is always there, always available, always what determines the course of natural events. The beavers simply use the water to their advantage.

Beaver ponds are lifelines for many species, and watching the comings and goings of the inhabitants of one can be highly instructive. Perhaps the most famous beaver-pond watcher of all was Henry David Thoreau, whose writings of life by Walden Pond have inspired countless people to consider, or reconsider, their roles in nature.

Cedar Swamp

Walking across an abandoned meadow, with the dried skeletons of last year's grasses poking at my legs, I hardly seem to be exploring a wetland. Yet my path along this gently descending slope is the same taken by the melting snow of spring and the fallen raindrops of summer. Down, down it leads, to the dark, damp, mysterious cedar swamp in the distance. Foreboding to look at from afar, the cedar swamp is actually a place of great beauty and much life.

When determining wetland types, certain plants can be used as indicator species, species that proclaim "water is near." Cedars are one, as are cattails, tamaracks, and sedges. Even in the drought of summer you can locate a wetland simply by knowing what plants to look for; the water may lie just below the soil's surface, waiting, nourishing, creating life.

At the wall of cedars that mark the edge of this wetland, I twist by outstretched branches, duck under higher ones, and enter the enchanting swamp. Cedar swamps are different from other treed swamps in that the water is difficult to see. It's present, but below the spreading layer of roots. Hardwood swamps and beaver-flooded swamps have water, water everywhere; cedar swamps have only damp black soil. But cedar swamps are a botanical wonderland. Lush stands of ostrich fern crowd their perimeter, needing sunlight to survive, yet dying if exposed too long. Next are the scattered patches of sensitive and royal ferns, but they soon disappear as you reach the interior of the swamp.

The floor of this wet woods never dries out, because of the screening effect of the thick evergreen branches. Since the ground is so shaded and so wet, special plants grow there that are not found in any other habitat.

The reptilian-looking leaves of liverwort cling to the tree roots that protrude from the hidden vault of moisture. Mosses mingle around these flat, scaly leaves, and tiny shoots of new growth push forth in search of light. My footprints fill in rapidly with water, and I am reminded to tread gently so as not to disturb the ground any more than is absolutely necessary. Layers of vegetation rely on one another for protection, nutrients, and support. Colonies of one species cluster in isolated stands, surrounded by an undulating landscape of mosses.

To really see the complexities of this community you have to get your knees wet, for low and up close is how to view this habitat. Green-stalked wildflowers, supporting green blossoms, grow against

Two orchids, early coralroot (above) and heart-leaf twayblade, require visits from male mosquitoes to become pollinated. While common to most cedar swamps, the wildflowers can be difficult to spot because of their superb camouflage.

FACING PAGE: Growing wherever it can find a dry foothold, the bunchberry adds an elegant touch to the cedar woods. When the berries ripen in the fall, mice, ruffed grouse, and deer will consume them.

The haunting call of the barred owl is a usual nighttime sound in the swamp. The only owl with brown eyes, it hunts for mice, voles, and cottontail rabbits along the edges of the wetland.

a mottled green background, and are often overlooked. Overlooked by us, perhaps, but sought out and easily discovered by insects, which find them by scent. The tiny one-leaf rein orchid and heart-leaved twayblade are two common, yet difficult-to-spot, plants of the cedar swamp. To locate them you must either place your head level with the damp mosses and look sideways along the Lilliputian horizon, or be a male mosquito.

Mosquitoes certainly are a part of this habitat, but you can gain some consolation in that only half the population is biting you. The females must have a blood meal to acquire the protein they need to produce eggs, but the males feed only on flower nectar. Without mosquitoes, several species of plants would not even exist!

Calls from birds echo through the green swamp—the melodious warble of a wood thrush is answered by the cries of an ovenbird; the musical whistle of a white-throated sparrow follows the nasal notes of a white-breasted nuthatch. Here in the "quiet woods" it is seldom quiet. Mates must be attracted, territorial boundaries declared, food claimed, and warnings issued.

Another call resounds throughout the swamp, mixing with another, then another. It is the diminutive spring peepers, their chorus of shrill peeps travelling about a kilometre through the air. Wood frogs, with their black-masked faces, have a subtle quacklike call, and are found in almost every pool of cool water that appears between the roots of the towering cedars.

An ancient hemlock survives on a small island within the swamp. The mauve-barked tree was too small to log years ago and is too diseased to be of any "value" to any logger today. But it is just right for a rather large, sleepy porcupine. The hollow trunk opens wide at the base, the entrance littered with the aromatic, peanut-shaped droppings of the resident. The hemlock's stout branches are ideal sunning spots, and the new, growing tips provide a ready meal. Porcupine perfection.

Throughout this swamp burst the blossoms of lady's-slipper orchids, both yellow and showy, mixed with the blooms of gaywing, bunchberry, moccasin flower, and one-flowered wintergreen. Here is a botanical treasury, scattered and hidden, waiting for someone to discover and appreciate it.

Living comfortably within the cedar forest is the snowshoe hare. Its fur turns colour and varies in density with the seasons. In autumn, the fur on its large hind feet becomes thick and long, so that the hare leaves behind an oversize, or snowshoe-shaped, footprint.

Using the landing pad of a yellow lady's-slipper orchid, this crab spider waits in ambush for the next bee to visit. The spiders come in two colours, yellow or white, and must find flowers of a like colour if they hope to have any success in their hunting.

Because willows can survive while partially submerged, wetlands and willows go together. Everyone has collected pussy willows in the spring, but not everyone realizes that they later turn into these beautiful flowers. Honeybees are attracted to willow flowers because they are among the first plants to bloom each spring.

Ferns grow in thick profusion just inside the boundary of a cedar swamp. Ostrich fern (left) and maidenhair fern love the moist soils and filtered sunlight in this part of the habitat.

Seldom seen but common to wet areas is the star-nosed mole. It burrows easily through the loose organic soil with its oversize front paws to locate the many grubs it eats daily.

Etched among the mosses are a few well-worn game trails—the highways and byways of the swamp denizens. Snowshoe hare and white-tailed deer use and reuse these easily traversed passageways, packing the soil with each passing. Trappers, hunters, and photographers know the value in locating these obvious signs.

My walk has taken me in a wandering loop, and I emerge through the belt of cedars not far from where I entered. As I retrace my trail across the meadow, my shadow stretching longer than when I started out, and in the opposite direction, a barred owl calls behind me, its mellow tone setting the mood for the evening.

BOGS AND FENS
Walking on Water

Have you ever tried walking on water? How about time travel? If you're like everyone else I know, you probably haven't had much success with either venture. However, the next best thing is a visit to a floating bog.

Bogs are wet, mysterious places that filmmakers, storytellers, and writers have immortalized in their works, usually by having villains of all sorts live and/or die in them. Society has thus learned that bogs are good places to avoid.

Perhaps the stories were started to discourage children of long ago from playing near the dangerous mats of vegetation. Careless crossings often resulted in at least a good soaking. As people, carts, and livestock disappeared beneath the mosses and tangled shrubs, no wonder warnings had to be issued to avoid these areas.

Bogs were formed thousands of years ago; a beaver-created swamp, by comparison, is but an ephemeral wet spot in time. Most bogs began in the depressions left as the glaciers retreated. Huge blocks of ice broke off and remained behind. The weight of these ice blocks, and their meltwater, created deep ponds with a restricted flow of water.

Other bogs began when the land mass sprung upward as the weight of the glacier disappeared. Pockets of water became trapped as almost stagnant ponds. The deep, bowl-shaped holes, full of water that couldn't escape, set the stage for bogs to develop.

Vegetation started growing around the rim of the depression, but the depth of the water and its lack of nutrients prevented much growth from occurring in the water itself. Also, many bogs are situated on granite bedrock, a stone base that is acidic by nature, hence inhospitable to life.

Tamarack and black-spruce seedlings began to take root in the mossy banks of the bogs, and soon sent out rootlets in search of food. More moss, usually sphagnum, grew on these roots and eventually allowed more seeds to find a place to grow. Soon cranberries, leatherleaf, and sweet gale had a network of roots running through the sphagnum raft. As these grew toward the centre of the pond in an ever-tightening circle, the open water gradually became blanketed with this floating vegetation.

Low oxygen levels in the water (there is no underwater growth to create oxygen or wave action to mix water and air), coupled with high acid levels (the ponds are situated on igneous rock and are

Orchids usually prefer a slightly acidic soil, so bogs provide the white-fringed orchid and arethusa with the perfect place to put down roots. White-fringed orchids grow tall and showy, and are easily seen in bloom; arethusa (above) remains hidden, having a surprised look about it when discovered.

FACING PAGE: *Once the mat of floating vegetation is established—a process that takes a few centuries to complete— woody species begin to dominate. Black spruce and tamarack rise above laurel and leatherleaf, which provide shade to the sphagnum mosses, cranberries, and orchids.*

This ancient bog has been here long enough to support larger plants such as these tamarack. Nutrients are hard to come by in this habitat; as a result trees grow slowly. These trees, still narrow enough to wrap two hands around, are about eighty years old.

subject to acidic precipitation) make decomposition within a bog a very slow process. Also, only very few bacteria or other decomposing organisms are present. Dead leaves and sticks fall to the mat and provide some cover and food to the new seedlings, but under the mat little is added to create a substratum.

Over time, organic soil material called peat accumulates near the ancient shoreline. It takes five hundred years for a foot of peat soil to be created. Peat soils contain large amounts of sphagnum moss, both living and dead, and thus have excellent water retention. It is this characteristic that makes peat moss valuable to gardeners.

The spongy texture of this soil is what causes the bog to "quake," or gives you that "waterbed sensation" when you walk across the surface. Trees several metres away can sway from the undulations your body weight produces in the mossy mat.

Be careful when you explore a bog, both for its health and your own sake. It's easy to damage the fragile rootlets, and repeated visits can produce changes in the bog's micro-ecosystem. And there really

Tamaracks, or larches, are often mislabelled as evergreens because the trees lose their needles each year. Their proper designation is conifer, meaning they reproduce through seeds held in cones. The soft needle clusters grow each spring, adding another layer to their twigs. New cones appear as red rosebuds, which turn brown and harden through the summer months.

is the danger of breaking through the mat and disappearing below. A bog in Denmark was drained and mined for peat, and the remains of a man believed to be about two thousand years old were discovered. Because of the incredibly slow rate of decomposition in the bog, he appeared quite lifelike!

Scientists have found that the well-preserved bits and pieces found in peat can supply interesting information about the local area. Pollen grains, although microscopic, are easily identifiable as to plant species. By taking a core sample, it is possible to know which plant species dominated the surrounding area, and for how long. In the Great Lakes region, pollen records go back more than ten thousand years.

I was leading a field trip with a group who were discovering the value of wetlands and learning about the different types native to their region. When we arrived at the bog, an undefinable emotion arose within the group: not really fear, but perhaps trepidation. They all had heard or read those stories of "bog creatures" and knew that many people had been "swallowed whole" by bogs. Yet they certainly wanted to get in there and see what the place was all about.

We wove our way through the tamaracks, hopped from hummock to hummock of sedge, and finally resigned ourselves to getting wet as we entered the sphagnum zone. Wildflowers abounded—not all in bloom, but we recognized bog laurel, bog rosemary, leatherleaf, grass pink, and rose pogonia, and found the distinctively shaped leaves of sundew and pitcher plant scattered throughout.

White-fringed orchids.

Examining the laurel blooms more closely, we noticed that several "pollen traps" had been sprung. When the blossoms had first opened, each pollen-laden anther had been held taut against the petals. A bee landing to inspect the nectar at the centre of a bloom had tripped the anther, causing it to spring inward and the pollen grains to stick to the bee's back. No harm done to the bee, which had continued on to other blooms, tripping more anthers and transferring more pollen as it went.

We knew that peat accumulates at a rate of about one foot ever five hundred years. We had a three-foot core sampler with us, which would tell us the depth of the bog we were in. As the sharp bit of the device was pushed into the wet soil, a silence befell us. Down, down the sampler core went, until its handle rested deep in the green sphagnum. A quick twist, and the core sampler was pulled up, ever so slowly so that suction wouldn't rob us of any of this treasure.

When we laid the core sampler horizontally on the ground, all voices burst forth at once. There were exclamations over the varying shades of brown in the layers, and words of disappointment that the deepest section of the bit revealed only water. Then we methodically inspected the sample itself from surface layer to wet substratum.

Bits of root material, old leaves, and lots of moss dominated the top few inches, then the rest became an almost uniform band of semi-decayed organic materials. We took a chunk from the two-foot level and rubbed it apart to feel the coolness of the water (the air temperature was very hot) and experience the fibrous texture of this totally organic material.

In my little sample there was something small, edged, and hard. More rubbing and a splash of water exposed a seed, probably from a sedge. In a way it was expected—after all, we were in a wetland. But this seed had come from the near bottom of the sample, the two-foot mark—it was ten centuries old!

My thoughts raced through all I had learned in those history classes at school: the seed had been in the bog when my ancestors arrived from England in the 1840s; in fact, it had been there long before Christopher Columbus had gone looking for India. It was created about the same time Leif Ericson's boat bumped into L'Anse-aux-Meadows!

That was a long time ago; and there I was, holding it in my hand. Those history lessons suddenly became quite real.

Once again I could only marvel at what wonderful places bogs are. They are fragile, yet they have remained intact and have continued to function when so many other habitats have come and gone. Bogs hold secrets, are places where you can walk on water, and even, with a bit of imagination, do some time travelling. They are areas that demand respect, not just from the point of view of safety, but because they are our precious natural heritage.

A few bogs support floating rafts of cranberries—a delicious accompaniment to Christmas turkey. The demand for this wild food is so great that some companies have created their own bogs in which to grow this plant commercially.

Fields of Bulrushes

Fens are hot places. Since there is no vegetation overhead to offer shade, bright sunlight reflects off the water's placid surface, and heat becomes part of any fen outing.

Still, they are such exciting spots, so interesting biologically, that you overlook the discomfort. Rare plants lie literally underfoot, and birds, uncommon in other habitats, sing, hunt, and nest there. Mammal runways crisscross the brown mat of slowly decaying vegetation.

But fens are fragile places, and repeated visits will actually destroy them. Each footprint you make will stay for possibly decades, and pathways quickly become the base for a stream. To interrupt the delicate pattern of water flow is to change a fen forever.

As with bogs, whatever dies in a fen takes a long time to "go away." This is due to a combination of factors: slow inflow of water, the very low oxygen levels below the soggy surface, and the simple lack of bacteria. A core sample of a fen would show that vegetation exists from surface to bedrock; a bog, by comparison, is a floating mat of vegetation, with clear water eventually found at some depth.

All wetlands act as water reservoirs, but fens hold an incredible amount—3.2 million litres per hectare for every 30 cm of depth. A two-hectare fen just two metres deep could retain 42.9 million litres (almost 10 million gallons) of water!

Some biologists argue that fens are simply a developmental stage of a bog, others contend that fens are wetland types unto themselves. Generally, bogs are acidic in pH and have a floating mat of vegetation consisting of sphagnum moss, cranberry, black spruce, and tamarack; while fens are usually alkaline, with bulrushes, sedges, and wildflowers being the dominant vegetation. If a bog has formed near the limestone bedrock of southern Ontario, it may indeed display fenlike characteristics.

Nomenclature aside, fens are unique areas to explore, albeit lightly. Orchids such as twayblade, northern white, calopogon, and purple fringed grow there, and other wildflowers abound—yellow loosestrife with its showy blossoms, smooth rose, shrubby cinquefoil, grass-of-Parnassus, Kalm's lobelia, and small-flowered gerardia. Pitcher plant scatters itself everywhere, its tall flower stalks rising to oversee the coming and goings within the fen.

A member of the gentian family, the succulent buckbean is a special find in a fen or bog. Its three-part leaf is well hidden beneath the layer of the previous year's bulrush growth, and the flower head lasts only a few days before it wilts and turns brown.

FACING PAGE: A delicate beauty of the fen is the calopogan or grass pink orchid. The bloom is hinged at the middle, and for it to be pollinated, a bumblebee must bend the top section over, since the pollen sacs are waiting on the lower section. Successful pollination is rare, so colonies of these orchids seldom increase in size.

Alkaline ponds, such as those within a fen, are the breeding grounds for the red-spotted newt. The larval form has gills and stays underwater for the first summer. It then metamorphoses into a terrestrial form, called a red eft, for about two years. When ready to mate, it returns to the water, changes into an olive-green adult, and remains in the pond.

Nestled in the bit of moss that grows at the base of stunted cedar trees are the small rosettes of sundew. Three varieties of this charming meat eater sometimes exist in a fen: the common round-leaved sundew, the uncommon lance-leaved form, and the rare hybrid of these two, called spatulate-leaved sundew. All have tiny white flowers displayed on a single spray held above the vegetation mat, and all have the sticky red "hairs" on their leaves that can spell doom for any insect that alights for food or rest.

Pitcher plants, which thrive in either bogs or fens, are as exotic as the sundew in the way they gather their food. Their tubular leaves catch rainwater and dew, then produce a fragrant secretion to sweeten the pot. Lured by this concoction, insects alight on the glandular surfaces of the leaves, slip inside, and drown in the wet bait. Bacteria attack the carcasses, and the nutrients that are released are absorbed by the leaves.

It has taken botanists quite a while to understand this complex process of food gathering. In the mid-1700s a botanist named Catesby announced that the hollow leaves were actually places where insects could hide from frogs. Not until the early 1800s did the idea come forth that perhaps the leaves weren't shelters, but rather a means for capturing insects. In 1875, J.H. Mellichamp, a physician, and Sir Joseph Hooker, a botanist, conducted experiments with pitcher plants and discovered the intricate ways of this marvelous plant.

Both the sundew and the pitcher plant are well suited to survival in the wet, hot, nutrient-poor environment of a fen. With decomposition happening so slowly, most nutrients remain locked up in any dead plant matter. For both species to survive, alternative food sources had to be found; hence the evolution of their ability to capture and digest certain invertebrates. Now they have a well-balanced diet of water, nutrients within the water, and critters!

Also found in fens are two well-camouflaged species of arrowgrass, one tall and slender, with a tight clustering of flowers along the wandlike tip, the other short and delicate, with tiny complex flowers coloured to match the drab tans and browns of a fen's palette. Finding either is the highlight of a field-botanist's day.

Hardstem bulrushes are usually quite abundant in fens, their whiplike stems swaying in the gentlest of breezes. Their tassels of seeds, when ripe,

The round-leaved sundew, a species of meat-eating plant, catches insects with the sticky-tipped hairs on its leaves. As a blackfly struggles to free itself from the mucilaginous "dew," the leaf curls around it, secreting digestive enzymes. A few days later the leaf will reopen, the remains of its meal still visible.

Fens usually have a limestone base, so that the water is slightly alkaline, thus encouraging the growth of sedges and rushes. Because there is little diversity of nutrients, several plants, such as sundews, pitcher plants, and bladderworts, must capture insects to supplement their needs.

Cotton grass is a generic name given to any sedge with fluffy seeds. Sedges are an indicator species not only for a wetland, but for an alkaline one, and usually indicate a fen.

Even though large mammals may be absent or exist in low numbers, fens are home to many types of invertebrates. The black-and-yellow argiope makes her large web among the taller bulrushes, luring insects with her brightly coloured body. In the web are the midges that were caught overnight.

will attract red-winged blackbirds and migrating ducks. Meanwhile damselflies and dragonflies will use them as lookouts for the summer's duration. Nesting within the dense stands of bulrushes may be sedge wrens, uncommon at the best of times, or the larger marsh hawk, or perhaps a short-eared owl. Blue-winged teals and mallards often hide their down-lined nests within a fen.

Yellow swallowtail butterflies visit the beckoning blooms, as do myriad other flying insects. Mosquitoes usually avoid the open spaces of a fen on hot summer days, but bloodthirsty deer flies more than make up for their absence. To locate mosquitoes, just stick your head into a shrubby patch—you'll find hundreds, if not thousands, of them.

Leopard frogs stay all summer, enjoying the warm waters; green frogs prefer the cooler water of a marsh, and wood frogs favour the shaded confines of the conifers. Red-spotted newts and mole salamanders conduct their springtime courtships within the shallow pools of the fen.

Since the plants provide minimal shelter, compared with marsh or forest vegetation, few mammals live here. But the spongy organic soil reveals the trails of those that pass through: white-tailed deer, raccoons, coyotes, snowshoe hare, and the smaller voles and lemmings all travel established pathways.

When you first see a fen it looks little more than a flooded hayfield. Inspect it, however, and you'll find a world of life that will overwhelm you with its diversity, complexity, and subtle beauty.

The jungles of the world are home to plants with bizarre and amazing ways of providing food for themselves, but the pitcher plant of our fens and bogs is just as impressive. Insects crawl inside the plant's hollow water-filled leaves, where they drown in a bath containing digestive juices. As they decompose, their nutrients are absorbed by the plant.

Oh, the Problems

Wetlands—this one word means so much: life, diversity, clean water, cool water, stored water. In the natural scheme of things, there are no negative aspects to wetlands, since they provide the essentials all life needs to continue. Only when we change wetlands to benefit some scheme of our own do we encounter problems.

Historically, wetlands have been regarded as "bad" places, unknown places, places to avoid, and, when possible, places to destroy. The folly of such thinking has caught up with us, for water tables are dropping in many regions, recreational opportunities are fewer, and tourist dollars have been reduced, while costs for irrigation systems and flood and erosion controls have increased dramatically.

It is shocking that many municipalities have yet to recognize wetlands as the most valuable type of real estate around; many still consider wetlands "hazard land," unfit for civilization, unless someone has enough money to fill them in and make them "valuable." Our society has given video stores, doughnut shops, and milk stores a higher priority than a healthy ecosystem.

Here are some of the indignities our wetlands have suffered:

FILL. Shallow cattail marshes have been smothered by the tonnes of soil dumped on them as fill. Once the newly placed soil gets to a certain height above the water table, health and engineering officials give the okay to build structures on what was once "wasteland." The subsequent acres of pavement, asphalt shingles, storm sewers, septic beds, and manicured lawns do not support even a fraction of the life that once lived in the now-buried wetland.

LANDFILL. This is a nice word for dump. In the area of central Ontario where I grew up, every dump I remember was placed in or beside a wetland. Two assumptions seem to have underlain this approach: that wetlands were to be filled and made "useful," and that wetlands would filter the seepage and retain the harmful runoff. Both assumptions have proven to be dangerously wrong.

DRAINAGE FOR CROPLANDS. I like salads and hamburgers as much as the next person, and I grew up in an agricultural community, but I cannot condone the wanton destruction of our wetlands just to

FACING PAGE: A picture is worth a thousand words.

Ditches, especially straight ones, draw water from the land efficiently. These dug trenches work so well that by summer there may be no water left for trees or wells.

As flood waters recede, silt accumulates on river bottoms, destroying spawning beds. A few years before this picture was taken, the river was 2 metres deep here; now you can walk across it wearing only rubber boots.

grow grain to feed a few extra head of cattle.

Until recently the government paid landowners to drain their wetlands and turn them into working fields. Thousands of hectares of swamp and marsh disappeared for the sake of a few more pounds of beef. Now government has to subsidize farmers who need deeper wells or trucked-in water to maintain their crops. A few landowners even plug their tile drain system to hold water in the soil.

CHANNELLING. The quickest way to drain a large wet area is to dig a channel, or ditch, through the lowest section. Snowmelt and rainfall shoot along this channel and are removed before they get a chance to soak into the surrounding soil. The straighter and deeper the ditch, the faster the water is removed.

EROSION. Downstream riverbanks have quickly felt the brunt of the uncontrolled onslaught of water that channelling produces, and erosion has become a serious concern in many areas. The accumulating silt is carried by the rushing turbulence to whatever final waterway it meets. Today it is commonplace to dredge canals through deposited silt to regain access to river systems.

PEAT EXTRACTION. Almost every bog in southern Ontario that could be drained has been drained. The rich organic soils, created over the past ten centuries or so, are mined as gardening soil. Pretty flowers have taken precedence over precious habitat.

POLLUTION. This problem is widespread, of course, but wetland habitats have felt the effects of unnatural contaminants the longest, simply because water runs downhill. Every chemical spill, every leaking septic system, every drop of landfill seepage, has eventually found its way into a wetland, poisoning it as effectively as if an assault had been planned.

As personal watercraft become affordable, the once-quiet bays and marshes turn into playgrounds for those ignorant of the delicate balances within these habitats. A simple cruise around a marsh may destroy that season's black-tern nests or spook the great blue herons from their colony.

Little spills of gas and oil, usually accidental, quickly add up to a problem. Fortunately, some wetlands are protected from the abuses of outboard motors.

EUTROPHICATION. This is a fancy word for overabundant plant growth. As agricultural and residential fertilizers are carried into a wetland, the plants of the area absorb them and grow higher, thicker, and greener than ever before. The wetland reaches a point where it cannot assimilate the introduced chemicals as fast as it can eliminate them; the result is a clogged system. Plant and wildlife diversity then drop dramatically.

ACCESS ROADS. As the demand for recreational sites increases, new roads are created to reach cottages or angling, hunting, and camping areas. Today such roads are studied and implemented with great care; a few years ago little thought was given to direction, construction, or impact. Streams were blocked with fill, undersized culverts were installed, and annual road-rebuilding projects occupied the time of municipal road crews and cottage associations.

URBAN SPRAWL. Subdivisions have eaten up huge areas of once-productive farmland; now the only sites left to build on are the wetlands. Municipalities do not protect them as green space, and the small ponds and streams soon disappear, to be replaced by storm sewers.

OVERTAXED RECREATIONAL AREAS. Because wetlands are productive areas and aesthetically rewarding places to visit, they are literally being used to death. That so few remain in heavily populated areas is contributing to their demise, because everyone wants his or her own "wilderness experience."

As a monument to their outing, some recreationists leave fishing lure boxes, candy wrappers, beer bottles, pop cans, plastic shotgun shells, sandwich bags, and the guts and scales from the day's catch at the access points to an area. Latrine pits seem to be unheard of by some folks. These inconsiderate individuals come from every outdoor user group, and although they are not many in number, they have ruined some areas for everyone, including themselves.

FEW PROTECTIVE LAWS. It is both amazing and shameful that until 1992, there was no legal policy in place in Ontario to protect wetlands. Prior to this any landowner could fill, dredge, or alter the wetland on his or her property. Now wetlands of provincial, regional, or local importance have limited protection from development. However, if a wetland has not been inventoried and classified, it may still suffer from abuse.

A few municipalities have followed recommended guidelines for developing sites near wetlands, but these guidelines are just that—guidelines, not law. Fish habitat has been protected for many years, shoreline alteration has been regulated, stream flow diversion has to be approved, but the "simple" marsh has no development restrictions placed on it, much to the delight of some landowners.

Because wetlands are so important to all of us, and because so few remain, it is time to impose limits on what people may or may not do with their property.

As if the aforementioned problems didn't place enough of a burden on our wetlands, along comes another one, natural in origin but introduced to North America from Europe in the early 1800s.

PURPLE LOOSESTRIFE. *Lythrum salicaria*, as the botanists call it, has invaded and destroyed large areas of once-productive wetlands. Originating in Europe, this pretty wildflower quickly established itself along the waterways of the northeastern United States. Because it has no predators, it spread steadily westward, into wet meadows and shallow marshes, shading and crowding out all native species of plants.

This particular species of loosestrife is incredibly hardy. It has withstood floods, severe freezing, drought, and even mutilation, which is how people first tried to curb its spread. Unfortunately, every severed rootlet, every chopped-up piece of stem, can regenerate a new plant.

As the clumps of loosestrife grow, the tall stems and bushy leaves create heavy shade, something the native, more delicate, wildflowers cannot tolerate. The stems of loosestrife are tough, almost woody, and the dead stems do not release stored nutrients back into the soils as quickly as the more herbaceous plants, which rot quickly.

Once purple loosestrife establishes itself, it is difficult to control and impossible to eradicate. Chemical sprays have had little lasting effect. Simply pulling it out is possible only in small areas, and only if done before large root systems are established.

There are currently plans to introduce three species of purple-loosestrife-eating insects from Europe into our North American ecosystem. Concerns have been raised about what else these beetles and weevils might dine on, but they are being addressed. The project looks promising, and may indeed be the salvation of many wetlands.

I have not mentioned all these problems to discourage you from enjoying wetlands; just the opposite. Once you are aware how important wetlands are, both to wildlife and to people, and become educated about the problems facing these habitats, then perhaps you can take action to ensure that wetlands remain viable areas and an intimate part of our lives.

While pretty to look at, purple loosestrife is rapidly choking the life from our wetlands. Growing in tall, dense clumps and having hard-to-decompose woody stems, this plant is claiming wetlands for itself. Attempts to control its spread have so far been unsuccessful.

Wetland Management

Instituting wood-duck boxes is probably the single most successful project undertaken to aid a species and has enabled this duck's population to rise from near extinction to the point where wood ducks are now abundant. Many other cavity-nesting species, such as the hooded merganser, bufflehead, goldeneye, screech owl, and flying squirrel, have benefited from this program.

FACING PAGE: Lush stands of bur marigold grow from dormant seeds during a drawdown of a marsh. In autumn, flocks of migrating songbirds and waterfowl will descend to dine on the ripe seeds.

The previous chapters have shown us that wetlands are valuable, indeed essential, to all forms of life, including people. That so many wet areas have been destroyed in the past is embarrassing, that we continue to destroy the few wetlands that are left is inexcusable.

The marshes, swamps, bogs, fens, and shorelines that remain around the lower Great Lakes must be protected from adverse development, rehabilitated where possible, and managed to ensure that their natural functions continue for centuries to come. To successfully manage a wetland is a complex task that often demands the combined skills of biologists, botanists, engineers and hydrologists.

It is not enough to create a management plan that is species specific; to manipulate a marsh only for the benefit of muskrats or mallard ducks—or stormwater runoff—is shortsighted and perhaps impossible. Such a strategy must take into account the potential for all wetland species indigenous to the site and be aware of the effects on connected habitats in the ecosystem.

As an example, Ducks Unlimited is one organization that has raised millions of dollars to fund the maintenance and enhancement of millions of hectares of wetlands and surrounding habitat. While preservation of waterfowl species is their rallying call, the real work of Ducks Unlimited is in the management of plant communities that provide quality habitat for the wide diversity of species dependent on wetlands.

As I said in the preface, I have worked at two major wetland sites in southern Ontario, Wye Marsh and Tiny Marsh. They are sister wetlands, both being about 800 hectares in size and on the same watershed. Wye Marsh is in a valley, surrounded by farms, a village, and industrial malls. Over the years, this marsh has been slowly choking on the effluent of its neighbours.

Tiny Marsh, surrounded by farms and forested land, has also suffered, being ditched, drained, farmed, and abandoned. But since 1967, Tiny Marsh has been intensively managed, and it outshone Wye Marsh in the clarity of its water and the diversity and abundance of its wildlife.

Managing wetlands also means managing the wildlife species that live there. When overpopulation threatens, harvesting programs, such as trapping or hunting, are implemented. These programs have strict guidelines, and are altered to match the wildlife population with the available habitat.

In 1990, a management program was prescribed for Wye Marsh. This once-dying wetland, its systems clogged with all manner of nutrients, silt, and chemicals, has been rejuvenated, and now produces clear water and supports wildlife species both rare and common. Wetland management works.

Management techniques range from the simple to the complex. Some are inexpensive; others demand hundreds of thousands of dollars. Whatever their cost, the theme of any management program is habitat enhancement—ensuring that proper amounts of food, water, shelter, and living space exist.

Here are examples of the management techniques employed at Tiny and Wye marshes and designed to benefit both wetland and wildlife:

To help ducks avoid predators, nesting baskets are placed in the marsh. Raccoons may swim out to these structures but are unable to climb the steel poles. Larger-diameter baskets can be used by geese.

DAMS. Typically, the first move in managing a wetland is to control the flow of water and the water levels. This is done by placing dams at key locations, with movable stop logs to maintain the desired water depth. Sometimes this is the only technique that needs to be employed—management is just a matter of holding water to support the life that needs it.

DYKES. These are long dams that divide a wetland into manageable sections. Water levels may differ on either side of a dyke, depending on what species are being managed for and what their water requirements are.

DITCHES. This sounds out of place in a discussion of management techniques, since I've said that ditches destroy wetlands, but these are different. Underwater ditches provide open water and corridors for fish, beaver, and otter; level ditches cut through thick cattail growth also provide open water for wildlife.

DRAWDOWN. Probably the most dramatic—and most misunderstood—technique, a drawdown duplicates what happens naturally in a beaver pond. Typically, there is a flood, and abundant food is available; as the food is eaten and becomes harder to find, the beavers leave and the dam eventually breaks; new growth prospers in the accumulated silt of the old pond; other beavers arrive and flood the area, eating the new growth. A drawdown recreates this

Cattails are an important element of a marsh, but dense stands do not permit a diversity of species. Creating openings within this jungle allows more species to use more area. The channels that are cut are called level ditches, but they are not for drainage. Random cuts are made with a snowblower-like machine called a cookie cutter; precise patterns can be achieved with a dragline.

fifty-to-sixty-year cycle, but on a compressed basis.

In a drawdown, the stop logs are removed from a dam in April, allowing the spring water to drain away. The dam remains fully open all summer, exposing the previously flooded area to air and sunlight. Oxygen in the air increases the rate of decay of the old marsh bottom; sunlight warms the damp soil and germinates dormant seeds, which use the suddenly released nutrients from the decaying vegetation. The marsh becomes a sea of green over the summer months. By early fall the stop logs are replaced and the marsh is reflooded, and will remain so for many years.

The result is abundant food, water, and shelter for wildlife. The following year the other side of the dam may be drawn down, but an adjacent area of normal water level is always maintained.

NESTING ISLANDS. These are expensive, but important if no other islands exist. Used by Canada geese, mallards, and teals, the islands often become home for killdeers, song sparrows, and yellow warblers. Migrating shorebirds will congregate on the gravel shores of these islands.

PONDS and POTHOLES. Openings within the dense stands of bulrushes, cattails, and canary grass are sought by waterfowl, marsh wrens, and muskrats. Either dug or blasted, these small ponds provide a wet oasis in a jungle of vegetation.

NESTING BOXES. These are easily added to any wetland, and there are a myriad of designs to choose from, depending on which species is being assisted. Wood ducks, buffleheads, hooded mergansers, screech owls, and flying squirrels all live in cavities near a wetland and make use of nesting boxes.

NESTING BASKETS. These are more difficult to make and maintain than nesting boxes, but they help mallards, blue-wing teals, and Canada geese to avoid nest predators such as mink and raccoons.

Two years before this photograph was taken, this chunk of field was almost lifeless; because a pond was dug, life now abounds. This blue-winged teal nested nearby; now her brood enjoys the shelter and food that naturally established itself around the pond.

To provide nesting sites for birds that prefer the solitude of a marsh to the dangers of a field, nesting islands are created. Sown with a mixture of ground cover and food crop, these islands attract waterfowl, songbirds, and shorebirds.

OSPREY POLES. Osprey are fish-eating hawks that raise their young in huge nests located near wetlands. The ability of these birds to reproduce has suffered because chemicals such as DDT have made their way into the food chain. As the environment is cleaned up, these birds are making a comeback.

Nest poles can be erected using old hydro poles, or pallet boxes can be attached to the tops of existing trees. Once a nest is established, the osprey will use it again and again, for many years.

HARVESTING. Hunting and trapping can be considered management techniques in that they manipulate populations of wetland wildlife. Once a good habitat is established, it becomes important to maintain animal populations at a level suitable to the habitat.

Left on their own, muskrats and beavers could establish their own population limits. But their populations would rise then fall dramatically, since overpopulation leads to food shortages and higher risk of diseases. During years of low populations, there is the added risk that a disease could decimate the species.

To maintain a fairly constant population, trappers harvest a set quota of animals, usually an estimation of the number that would die naturally over the winter. By removing some animals, the survivors have ample food, shelter, and living space to make it through the winter. Depending on how successful breeding is the next spring, new quotas may be set for the following autumn.

In the summer, ducks go through a complete moult, which renders them flightless for a few weeks. During this time of feather renewal, they must be able to sun themselves, find food, and avoid predators. They require loafing areas, logs or gravel islands within the stands of cattails or bulrushes, where they can moult undisturbed.

NORTH AMERICAN WATERFOWL MANAGEMENT PLAN (NAWMP). While ducks and geese are certainly the drawing card of this program, wetlands involved with NAWMP projects sustain much more than just waterfowl.

NAWMP is mandated to study and act on the key problems facing wetlands. Its many member agencies are concerned with long-range land use, declining waterfowl populations, and the misuse and abuse of wetlands.

Millions of dollars are allocated to projects where the loss of a habitat is imminent. The tasks of land acquisition, fundraising, planning, and site management are divided among the member agencies according to what each does best; but they all work together for a common cause: saving wetlands.

Wetlands and Education

Clearly, the wetlands that remain in the lower Great Lakes region are worth saving. The way to save them is through a three-part program: legislation, active management, and education. Wetlands must be protected by law, they must be maintained as ecologically healthy areas, and we can do this through education.

Once you understand how a wetland works—how important it is to people, wildlife, plants, and water cycles—it becomes difficult to sign its death warrant. Appreciation, understanding, and action are the routes to follow, paths blazed by meaningful education.

Children today are learning about environmental ethics and the negative effects our lifestyles are having on the planet. They are tackling issues in elementary school that many adults didn't consider until college or university. The fragile nature of our environment is evident, but the desire to sustain our environment is also apparent.

Working as a naturalist at two education centres whose programs deal specifically with wetland ecosystems, I've found that the students, teachers, and parents who visit these sites usually become quite excited about swamps and marshes, since life is everywhere and easily found.

The students in particular have incredible powers of observation. Whereas I might walk past a screech owl sleeping on a pine bough, or a grey tree frog snuggled in the crotch of an alder, or a water snake sunning on a log, at least one sharp-eyed student will spot it.

Children are naturally fascinated by the world around them, but traditionally we adults have stifled this interest. "Don't touch that!" "Put that down!" "Leave that alone!" How often did we, as children, hear those phrases over and over when we discovered frogs, snakes, bird nests, beetles, and bones. How often have we, as adults, said those same words to our children?

Give a child a dip net and the world of nature becomes intriguing. Crude swings of the net and cursory looks are soon replaced by fine handling and lengthy inspections of tiny creatures. Life is everywhere, in every scoop of the net.

FACING PAGE: Guided canoe trips, with a naturalist who can point out highlights that may escape a novice's eyes, are a wonderful way to explore a wetland. Not all education centres offer this service, so take advantage of any that do. This scene is from the Wye Marsh, near Midland, Ontario.

Expensive to construct and maintain but worth the cost when protection of the marsh is coupled with invaluable learning experiences, boardwalks allow marsh visitors a unique look at a wetland. Virginia rails, soras, bitterns, snapping turtles, and mink might be viewed or heard with just one early-morning stroll along a boardwalk.

Several years ago, a grade seven class was accompanying me along a nature trail that threaded through a thick swamp. The group was discovering, with great interest, green frogs, water lilies, ducklings, and beaver sticks. As we walked we listened to the yellow warblers competing vocally with the song sparrows for nesting territories.

On this particular hike there were three girls who just had to be out in front, and no amount of gentle coaxing could persuade them to join the rest of the pack. They stayed ahead of us by about twenty-five metres, far enough to feel independent, yet close enough to feel secure that we would save them if they found themselves under attack from a vivid imagination.

The trio had disappeared around a bend in the trail, when we heard a scream. I looked up just as a great blue heron gained enough altitude to clear the thick alders. At the same time, three blurs resembling students came shooting back down the trail.

"It was huge!" shrieked the first.

"It was so big!" gasped the second.

"It was right in front of us! We didn't even see it until it came up right in front of us!" shrieked the third.

When I asked them what "it" was, they had no idea. They weren't even sure that it was a bird. All they knew was (a) it was big and (b) it flew. After delving into their memory banks, they unanimously deduced an identification: pterodactyl! This led to another hearty round of gasping and shrieking.

Not one child in this group of twelve-year-olds, all reasonably intelligent, had even heard of a great blue heron! Yet they knew about dinosaurs, what they looked like, and many of their names. That upsets me. Rather than studying their natural environment, which they are a part of, they had been studying extinct reptiles. For a child to be knowledgeable about a long-gone dinosaur while uninformed about a common wetland bird was most disheartening.

Fortunately this has changed. Today, as we enter—at long last—an era of environmental awareness and appreciation, students are studying the interrelationships of living species, including humans. Supplementary programs are available to assist teachers with almost any topic of concern. Wildlife

A pterodactyl? No, but many children, and some adults, cannot identify a great blue heron, one of the most easily identifiable birds of a wetland. Great blue herons are mistakenly called cranes by many, or "blue herrings." The mislabelling of this majestic bird points to the desperate need for better education about our wetlands.

issues, forest-management and fisheries work, acid rain, endangered species, soils, and wetlands can be explored through music, art, science, math, and physical-education classes. Imagine how well the students who participated in these programs will make informed decisions when it is their turn to lead.

We, the elders of society, must teach the next generation about the wonders, diversity, and importance of the living world. If not, I fear a time will come when great blue herons, and those who watch them, will be as extinct as the pterodactyls.

As I lead children and adults into the world of a wetland, I see a magic take hold of them. The children become eager and interested, and their enthusiasm soon dispels the crusty indifference of so many adults. All it takes is a shriek of delight when a tadpole, dragonfly nymph, or minnow turns up wriggling in a dip net, and the adults are drawn from the sidelines into the circle of exploration and discovery.

When the time comes to end the session, my problem is not always with getting the children calmed down and reorganized, but with the moms and dads. They are the ones still wading knee-deep through the cattails and duckweed, trying to use the dip net "just one more time." What they are capturing is not so much the skittering water strider but a delicious memory from their youth.

Wetlands do that to you. They are magical places. They are places to visit the past and see the future; they are to be explored, appreciated, and protected.

Its shell chipped by thrown rocks, this rare spotted turtle has survived an attack by a group of adventure seekers. Empathy for wildlife will only come with understanding, which is the goal of education. Today they throw rocks at a turtle; tomorrow they may dump chemicals into the river.